Lost Tribes Institute's 2nd International Symposium; Chiang Mai, Thailand (May 9-10, 2024)

Theme: Ethnic Karen and the Hill Tribes

A Collection of Essays from International Researchers on the Ancient Link between Israel's Lost Tribes and Southeast Asia's Hill Tribes.

Chinag Mai, Thailand (May 9-10, 2024)

Cover by Richard Hewitt of attendees wearing ethnic Karen shirts
Shirts worn by men and women with fringes or tassels
Like the tzitzit that Jewish men wear in response to the following verse:

"Hashem said to Moses as follows: Speak to the sons of Israel and say to them [that they must] make for themselves *tzitzit* upon the corners of the clothes for generations, and on the *tzitzit* give a string of *techelet*. And they shall have for themselves *tzitzit* and they will see them and they will remember all of the commandments of Hashem and they will do them, and they will not stray after their hearts and eyes so that they shall not pursue after them. So that they will remember and adhere to all of my commandments and will remain holy to their God. I am Hashem your God who took you out of the land of Egypt to be for you a God. I am Hashem your God." Numbers 15:37-41, Sefaria Community Translation.

ISBN: 978-1-959466-12-3
Paperback

Published by Lost Tribes Cafe & Lost Tribes Institute (2024)

Lost Tribes Institute

Lost Tribes Institute's 2nd International Symposium

Table of Contents

A Vision for Manassites by Symposium Host, PS Haokip	3
Keynote Presentation: Karen – Lost Tribes of Israel by Margot Crossing	5
Video Message From Central Asia to Southeast Asia By Damir Eraliev	36
Israelites Who Migrated to Ancient Japan by Arimasa Kubo	39
Hata Clan by Dr. Kengo Nagami	49
Israelite Migrations Across Asia (Korea & SE Asia) by Howard Ha-Sung Chung	52
Ethnic Mizos in Northeast India, Myanmar and Bangladesh - Recognized in Israel as 'Bnei Menashe' by Dr PC Biaksiama	69
A Book for All Peoples by Richard Hewitt (Risbek)	76
Iconic Bible Chapters about Israel's Return by Richard Hewitt (Risbek)	79
Did Ancient Israelites Form Eastern Religions? (Part I) By Richard Hewitt (Risbek)	91
Schedule: Thailand Chiang Mai Symposium - Bones Come Together	110

A Vision for Manassites by Symposium Host, PS Haokip
Chiang Mai Symposium (May 2024)

A Vision for the Manassites: Bridging Ancient Heritage with a Flourishing Future

1, Mr. PS Haokip, as the host of this year Chiang Mai's Symposium, it was indeed both an honor and a privilege to bring together scholars, community leaders, and descendants of Manasseh from around the globe.

The Symposium was born out of a profound respect for the historical and cultural significance of the Manassites, one of the ten lost tribes of Israel. It serves as a platform to explore our rich heritage, celebrate our unique identity, and forge a vision for the future that is grounded in the wisdom of our ancestors yet vibrant with contemporary relevance.

Why Host the Symposium?
The decision to host this Symposium stemmed from a deep-seated belief in the power of community and the importance of preserving our collective memory. The Manassites, like many of the lost tribes, have a history that is both storied and fragmented. By hosting this event, we aim to piece together the fragments, rekindle a shared sense of identity, and inspire the next generation to take pride in their roots.

In an age where cultural homogenization threatens the uniqueness of distinct groups, it is imperative to provide a forum for the Manassites to reconnect with their past and discuss their future. This Symposium is not merely an academic exercise; it is a living testament to our resilience and commitment to ensuring that the legacy of Manasseh continues to thrive.

Our Vision:-
Our vision for the Manassites is twofold: 1) to honor our ancient heritage, and 2) to build a thriving, cohesive community that can navigate the complexities of the modern world.

1. Honoring Our Heritage:
We envision a future where the history and traditions of the Manassites are meticulously preserved and widely celebrated. This includes:
A. Historical Research: Encouraging scholarly research to uncover and document the history of the Manassites, filling gaps in our collective knowledge.
B. Cultural Revival: Promoting the revival of ancient customs, languages, and rituals that define our identity.
C. Educational Initiatives: Establishing educational programs and institutions dedicated to teaching the history and culture of the Manassites to younger generations

2. Building a Flourishing Community

While honoring our past is crucial, we must also look forward. Our vision encompasses creating a vibrant, interconnected global community of Manassites who are empowered to thrive in the 21st century. This includes:

A. Global Networking: Fostering a global network of Manassites to support one another through cultural, professional, and personal connections.

B. Innovation and Leadership: Encouraging Manassites to take on leadership roles in various fields, blending traditional wisdom with modern innovation.

C. Community Development: Investing in community development projects that enhance the quality of life, including healthcare, education, and economic opportunities.

Conclusion

The Manassites are a people of enduring spirit and rich history. Hosting this Symposium is a step towards ensuring that our heritage is not only preserved but also celebrated and integrated into the broader tapestry of human culture. Together, we can honor the legacy of Manasseh while crafting a future that is bright and full of promise. As we gather to share knowledge, forge connections, and inspire action, let us remember that we are the stewards of a remarkable legacy -The Manassites are Chosen among the Chosen, inheritors of the double portion blessing - a community Doubly Blessed by the Lord.

It is our collective duty to honor our ancestors by building a community that reflects their strength, wisdom, and resilience. Through unity and shared purpose, the descendants of Manasseh will continue to thrive, contributing to the richness of global diversity and the progress of humanity.

(PS Haokip)
Chief Patron, Manasseh Asia Foundation

Keynote Presentation: Karen – Lost Tribes of Israel
by Margot Crossing

The Golden Book and Other Traditions

Contents

Introduction

Early contact with British diplomat

Lost Book and a White Brother (Judson's servant)

Missionary quotes regarding Dr & Mrs Mason

Dr Mason's papers from Calcutta Christian Observer

Isaiah 11 and the four Karen *thah* (songs)

Reverend Baw Ney and the Golden Book

The Golden Book and other 'Lost Books"

Don Richardson

Dr McGowan and the Israelites of Chengdu

Torrance & the Ancient Israelites

Karen Founding Year – BC 739

Are the Karen alone as Israelites?

Dr Howard HS Chung and Manchu of China

Richard Hewitt and the Manas Epic

Map of Kyrgyzstan & Qiang 600 BCE

Maps of the Trade Routes – Horse Tea routes

Conclusion

Bibliography

Introduction

There still exists a significant amount of writings on the Karen from the nineteenth century. John Trew and Dr McGowan, among others, mention the findings of Dr and Mrs Mason who lived among the Karen in 1830's in Burmah (modern-day northern Myanmar). Dr Mason, at first, presumed their knowledge of the creation, the fall and the future regeneration of man, resulted from earlier contact with the Portuguese. When asked by a gentleman at the Civil Service to confirm this theory, Dr Mason set about collecting Karen traditions. Dr Mason writes of this inquiry that it "resulted in the irresistible conviction, contrary to my preconceived opinions, that the scriptural knowledge of the Karens has not been derived from Christians, but from Israelites".[1]

The Karens expect a Karen king to return, bringing with him the idyllic notions of equity for the poor, happiness for mankind, and peace among ferocious beasts; not unlike the Davidic king in Isaiah chapter 11.

The tradition of the 'lost' Golden Book is another strongly held belief of the Karen, even up until modern times. A younger white brother was thought to have it and would one day return it.

Other people groups, adjacent to the Karen, also hold beliefs and have evidence that they too were once Israelites.[2] Closer geographically this list includes the Kuki, Mizo and Chin peoples in NE India and the western side of Myanmar; and the Ch'iang or Q'iang in Sichuan in the Min River Valley, China. Further away but, once long ago, part of a larger geographical region – are the Kyrgyz people – with their Epic of Manas and the numerous biblical parallels and concepts within its pages.

---

[1] Calcautta Christian Observer 1835 page 351 https://archive.org/details/calcuttachristia04unse/page/350/mode/2up Accessed 27/4/2024

[2] The Lost Tribes Institute and the Symposiums that have been and will be held in the future through this Academic Research vehicle will continue to prove the connections of Israelite peoples in Asia.

China also holds forgotten records of a greater Israelite community within its borders. Richard Hewitt and Dr.Ha-Sung Chung can bring perspectives on these last Israelite connections to the Karen people.[3]

Early Accounts of the Karen

& their expectations

In 1795 a British diplomat from the embassy in Rangoon visited a Karen village with a Burmese guide. The diplomat was instantly surrounded by Karen tribesmen, believing he was the prophesied white man who would return their lost book and free them from their oppressors. "Tell them they are mistaken" was the diplomat's reply.[4]

The English diplomat was followed by a Muslim traveler in 1816.[5] Although not white, they also asked if he had the book. He left them with a small book which he told them had writings about God. The priest, to whom it was given, wrapped it in muslin and the people began to worship it. Later, when the missionaries arrived they were shown the book. "It is a good book," they said "but it should not be worshipped."

Lost Book and a White Brother

The story of the Karen and Christianity is unequivocally connected to the expectations, long held, of a Lost Book and a white brother returning it. When the British arrived the Karen's curiosity was aroused – could

---

[3] https://arabaev.academia.edu/RichardHewitt; https://handong.academia.edu/HaSungChung;

[4] He recounted it to his superior, Lieutenant Colonel Michael Symes, who referred to it is his book, *"An Account of an Embassy to the Kingdom of Ava in the Year 1795"*, published in Scotland

[5] Eternity in their hearts by Don Richardson, page 68

this be the white brother? However, it was the white missionaries with the book in hand that really initiated one of the great stories of the nineteenth century.

It is told by Dr Mason in his book *"The Karen Apostle"*, and briefly by Don Richardson[6]. Adoniram Judson arrived in 1817 to Rangoon as an American Baptist missionary to preach to the Buddhist Burmese. There were so few converts that he turned to translating the bible into Burmese. One day he hired a Karen man, Ko Thah-byu[7], looking for work to pay a debt. Judson and the other staff introduced the gospel of Jesus Christ to him but he seemed slow to understand. "Then a change took place. Ko Thah-byu began asking questions about the origin of the gospel and about these "white strangers" who had brought the message – and the book which contained it – from the west."[8] About this time a missionary couple, George and Sarah Boardman, arrived to help Judson and they set up a school for illiterate converts. Ko Thah-byu threw himself into learning to read and became pre-occupied with the Bible and its message, for it had already dawned on him that he was the very first Karen to learn that the lost book had already arrived in Burma. When the Boardmans announced plans to go to Tavoy, in the panhandle of southern Burma, Ko Thah-byu asked if he could go with them. After arriving in Tavoy, Ko Thah-byu asked to be baptised and then set out into the hills of southern Burma. Each time he came to a Karen village he preached and nearly every Karen, within earshot, was amazed at the message and soon hundreds of Karen flocked into Tavoy to see for themselves the white bother with the book.

---

[6] Eternity in their Hearts; by Don Richardson chapter 2 pp83-86

[7] He had been a robber and had killed at least thirty men

[8] Richardson page 83

It is reported that he went onto other Karen villages in central Burma and preached there; barely taking a break – he died from his labours a few years later. The fires he ignited in the midst of his people are still ablaze two hundred years later.

Missionaries, Jonathan Wade and Francis Mason, experienced what George Boardman had; that is an overwhelming acceptance of their message as the 'white brother with the Lost Book'.

Missionaries Quote Dr & Mrs Mason

News of the Karen and their astonishing acceptance of Christianity stunned the Western world. Not only was it that the Karen had a prophecy that primed them for the gospel but it was that they also had many oral traditions and customs that were unmistakably biblical. Dr Francis Mason initially thought the biblical knowledge had come from the Portuguese but on further investigation realized that they could only be descendants of the Ten Tribes that had migrated into this part of the world. John Trew mentions Mason's findings in Mission Life Vol. V 1874 pages 563-578. He writes,

> *It is supposed by some that the Karens are part of the lost tribes of Israel. How numerous would be the members of these tribes were the sum of all who are set down as belonging to them told! It certainly is convenient when you meet with a people whom you cannot account for, to give "the lost tribes" the benefit of the doubt.*
>
> *There is, however, this to be said for the above-mentioned theory, that [564/565] Dr. and Mrs. Mason found very remarkable and accurate traditions regarding the creation, the fall, and future regeneration of man.*

George Moore devoted an entire chapter to the Karen and its Lost Tribes of Israel theory.[9] His book, *The lost tribes and the Saxons of the East and of the West, with new views of Buddhism, and translations of rock-records in India,* adds a chapter at the end due to the international interest in the Karen of Burma.

Dr Francis Mason's Calcutta Christian Observer Papers

The British presence in India allowed many missionaries to travel to that part of the world. William Carey was there and Joseph Wolffe had visited. The Calcutta Christian Observer was widely distributed and read. All the missionaries sent their findings to the CCO for distribution to the west. Dr Mason was no exception. In 1834 and 1835 Francis Mason entitled two of his papers *The Karens of Burmah a remnant of the Ten Tribes of Israel. No. I & No.III*

Mason writes "[after] collecting the Karen traditions, and the inquiries that ensued, [it] resulted in the irresistible conviction, contrary to my preconceived opinions, that the scriptural knowledge of the Karens has not been derived from Christians, but from Israelites ; and that for the following among other reasons :

1. Because the Karens are trusting in a Saviour who is to come, whereas, had they been taught by Christians, they would be trusting in one who has already come.

---

[9] https://archive.org/details/losttribessaxons00moor/page/358/mode/2up & https://www.academia.edu/117215872/Chapter_XVIII_of_George_Moores_1861_book

2. Because they trace their scriptural knowledge not to teachers, but through their fathers to God himself. Not a vestige appears of their ever having derived religious knowledge from foreigners; but, on the contrary, they always say, that "God gave them commands."

3. Because attributing their scriptural knowledge to the instruction of foreigners, is supposing an effect without an adequate cause. It exists as the national religion of different tribes, that, until the present generation, were almost constantly at war with each other, and separated by a difference of dialect, which prevents the language of the one from being understood by the other; among a people scattered abroad to an unknown extent over Siam, Martaban, and Burmah.

4. Because there is nothing peculiarly Christian in their traditions, in distinction from that which is Jewish. But had they derived their scriptural knowledge from Christians, it would have been nearly all peculiarly Christian. Both Catholic and Protestant Missionaries make the doctrines of Christ and the Cross the principal theme of their instructions; and for the converts of either persuasion, to forget the Cross, Baptism, and the Lord's Supper, and even that there ever was such an individual as Christ, while they remembered the formation of woman from man's rib, the dispersion at Babel, and the original purity of Satan, seems to be morally impossible. Yet not a vestige of the former can be discovered, while the latter are familiar to all.

5. Because there are many things peculiarly Jewish in the phraseology which is not Christian."[10]

---

[10] https://archive.org/details/calcuttachristia04unse/page/350/mode/2up Page 351

Mason published many findings but the two referencing the Ten Tribes of Israel are found in May 1834 and July 1835 journals.[11] The name of their God is of great interest, Mason writes on page 212, May 1834:

> *God is denominated the great Ku-tsa or the great Lord; the great Pu, or great ancestor from Pu a grandfather: — but his proper name is Yu-wah, and there can scarcely be a rational doubt but the Yu-wah of the Karens, is the Jehovah of the Hebrews.*

The following is a fragment obtained from a Siamese Karen. The same is meant by mountain height in this, as my new city in the piece in another song from page 217, and is decidedly a scriptural expression for the reinstatement of the Israelites in their own land.

> *"At the appointed time our father's Jehovah will return;*
> *Though the flowers fade, they bloom again.*
> *At the appointed year our father's Jehovah will return;*
> *Though the flowers wither, they blossom again.*
> *That Jehovah may bring the mountain height.*
> *Let us pray both great and small;*
> *That Jehovah may establish the mountain height,*
> *O matrons, let us pray.*
> *That Jehovah may prepare the mountain summit.*
> *Friends and relations, let us pray.*
> *You call yourselves the sons of Jehovah;*
> *How often have you prayed to Jehovah?*
> *You call yourselves the children of Jehovah;*
> *How many nights have you prayed to Jehovah?"* page 217 of May 1834

---

[11] https://www.academia.edu/117719511/Karen_of_Burmah_a_remnant_of_ten_tribes_of_Israel_by_Dr_Mason_Part_I_1834
https://www.academia.edu/117910900/
THE_KAREN_OF_BURMAH_A_REMNANT_OF_THE_TEN_TRIBES_OF_ISRAEL_Part_III_IBY_DR_MASON_Written_1835

The Karens believe that when they obtain a king, he will be sole monarch of the world, and that everyone will be happy. Rich and poor will not exist; much in accordance with the scriptural representation of the return of the Israelites.

> *"When the Karen king arrives,*
> *There will be only one monarch;*
> *When the Karen king comes,*
> *There will be neither rich nor poor;*
> *When the Karen king shall come,*
> *Rich and poor will not exist."*

They believe when the Karen king comes, the beasts will be at peace, and cease to bite and devour one another, in accordance with the Scripture view of the millennium.

> *"When the Karen king arrives,*
> *Every thing will be happy;*
> *When the Karen king arrives,*
> *The beasts will be happy;*
> *When Karens have a king,*
> *Lions and leopards will lose their savageness."*[12]

These songs cannot but remind the reader of Isaiah 11:6 and 65:25 *"The wolf and the lamb shall feed together, The lion shall eat straw like the ox, And dust shall be the serpent's food. They shall not hurt nor destroy in all My holy mountain," Says the LORD.* Is 65:25

---

[12] abid pages 217,218

Isaiah 11 and Four Karen *Thah* (songs)

In fact, Isaiah chapter 11 has four Karen '*thah*' or songs that relate directly to the meanings within that chapter. I was in a small Karen village preaching in their church. After showing that three Karen *thah*/songs matched Isaiah 11 perfectly in their meanings, an older woman shared that there is another *thah* that she knew that also matched Isaiah chapter 11. The older woman said that the *thah* said, "*a tree will be cut down, yet a shoot will come from the root and grow into a branch*"

We know that the root of Jesse is David and also the Davidic king or Messiah figure. Dr Mason writes that a Karen *thah*/song say:

> "God comes blowing the great trumpet [or trumpets].
> The great Doo [13] plays (or played) the golden harp."

He goes on to say that Doo[14] must mean David. Of course, we understand that the shoot of Jesse refers to David and also implies the Davidic Messiah. ISAIAH chapter 11:1

> "*A shoot will come out
> from the stump of Jesse,
> and a branch will bear fruit
> from his roots.*

The two Karen *thah* above relate directly to verses 4 and verses 6-8:

> *4 but with righteousness he will judge the needy,
> and decide with equity for earth's poor.*

---

[13] Doo, in the second line, may be easily derived from David, by w going into 'oo', and dropping the final consonant, according to the genius of the Karen language.

[14] Richard Hewitt was also at the Chiang Mai LTI Symposium and he said that the Kyrgyz say the name David as "Dood"

Here we see verse 4 relates directly to the meaning of the Karen *thah:*

When the Karen king shall come,
Rich and poor will not exist.

Verses 6-8 of Isaiah 11 speak about the beasts losing their savageness.

6 The wolf will live with the lamb;
the leopard will lie down with the young goat.
The calf and the lion will graze together,
and a little child will lead them.
7 The cow and the bear will graze,
and their young will lie down together,
and the lion will eat straw like the ox.
8 The nursing child will play
over the hole of the cobra,

Which has the same meaning as - *When Karens have a king,*
Lions and leopards will lose their savageness - in the *thah* above.

It is extraordinary to think that in the early 1800s, the Karen still remember a passage from the prophet Isaiah that they carried with them, in song, for over 2,500 years.

Could it be that they knew that the promise in Isaiah 11:12 of the dispersed or exiled of Israel returning from the ends of the earth was a promise to themselves as the remnant of the northern ten-tribe kingdom of Israel? Were they truly waiting for their promised king, the Davidic offspring of Jesse?

Isaiah 11:10-12

*10 At that time, as to **the root of Jesse**, who will be standing as a banner for the peoples, the nations will rally to him, and his resting place is glorious.*

11 At that time, the Lord will reach out his hand yet a second time to recover the remnant that is left of his people, from Assyria, from Lower Egypt, from Upper Egypt, from Cush, from Elam, from Shinar, from Hamath, and from the islands of the sea.

*12 He will raise a banner for the nations and will assemble **the dispersed of Israel**; he will gather the scattered people of Judah **from the corners of the earth**.*

Mason goes on to write that they do not practice Jewish rites like sacrifices to God or circumcision. Therefore, the conclusion must be made that if the Karen have gotten their biblical ideas from their forefathers and not white Christians; they have neither Christian nor Jewish rites, then they must have gotten these ideas from ancestors who undoubtedly are the exiled wandering Ten Tribes of Israel from 8th century BCE Assyrian exile.

These few songs quoted here reinforce that the Karen did indeed remember scripture but that their expectation of a coming king, rather than one who had already come, precluded them from having heard this from Christians. The only logical conclusion must be that they were ancient Israelites from the Assyrian captivity and relocation.

When the news of the Karen as a remnant of the Ten Tribes of Israel reached Britain, in the mid-1800s, it made quite a stir. "How could they have gotten there?" We now know of a growing body of evidence that other people groups, not too distant to the Karen, also carried songs, chants, and traditions that marked them as Ancient Israelites too. The

Lost Tribes Institute is building a catalog of presentations, like this paper, through the work of its researchers and the Symposiums that they put on. Reading Dr Mason's two articles in the Calcutta Christian Observer is highly recommended and the links are supplied at the end of this paper.

Reverend Baw Ney's Story & the Golden Book

One of the ways that the Karen apostles and evangelists used, to bring the message of the Kingdom of God, to the Karen tribesmen was through their traditional songs and chants. One such Karen was Baw Ney[15].

About 1935, when coming to a new village, Baw Ney would gather the children and sing traditional Karen songs for them. After he had the children's attention, he would teach them to sing the Karen songs and to read the Karen Bible. Soon the adults of the village would gather to see what was happening. It was at this time that Baw Ney recited traditional Karen poems and stories. One of the stories he always told was the ancient Karen story about the Golden Book of Life:

---

[15] http://thekarentribe.weebly.com/baw-ney.html Reverend Baw Ney was the founder of the village of Tee Mae Ker Lah. Today, at age 86, he lives with Kar Bu, his wife of 55 years, next to the Tee Mae Ker Lah Church that he pastored for more that 40 years. He was born in 1909 in Lampang, Thailand. Before he was born, Baw Ney's parents became Christians under the preaching of Karen missionaries from Burma. Written 1995

After Y'wa created the earth he decided to go on a long journey, and so he called his sons together and gave each a book of life. To the Karen, the eldest, he gave a Golden Book of Life. To the others he gave other books of life, until finally to the white man, the youngest brother, he gave a White Book of Life. The white brother took his White Book of Life and went away to the west, and was never seen again. As long as the Karen read and followed his Golden Book of Life, his life was happy and prosperous.

One day the Karen brother was burning and clearing a field in the forest. He put his Golden Book of Life on a stump in the field while he was doing his work. In his carelessness, the Golden Book of Life was burned, leaving only fragments that he brought back to his house. Gradually the older brother neglected these fragments, until one day they fell through the cracks of the bamboo floor in his house, and the pigs and chickens underneath ate them up.[16]

Of course, it was this 'lost book' and the anticipation of a younger white brother returning the book that set up the Karen for the missionaries in the early nineteenth century. Names like Dr Francis Mason, George Boardman, Mr Wade, and many others were the "younger white brother." Karen quickly spread the message 'that the fulfillment of their prophecy had arrived'. Ko Thah-byu, the Karen Apostle, was the first of many Karen that carried the message of the book to a wider and wider number of Karen villages. Rev Baw Ney was also one such amazing Karen.

---

[16] Karen Traditions & Christianity http://www.stolaf.edu/people/leming/film.htm#Scene3 Accessed 2014

Golden 'Lost Book' and Other Lost Books

Well, the Karen are not alone in their Lost Book tradition, nine other hill tribes in this region have similar oral traditions. [17]

'**The Kachin**, *like the Karen, believe that* Karai Kasang[18] *once gave their forefathers a book which they lost.*'[19]

The **Lahu** tradition say *Gui'Sha*[20] had given their ancestors a written law written on rice cakes and during a famine they were forced to eat the rice cakes for their survival.[21]

The **Wa** await a white brother with their Lost Book.[22]

The **Shan** and **Palaung** peoples look to a fifth manifestation of Buddha, known as *Phra-Ariya-Metrai*, who was spoken about in their scriptures that were lost in the war in Laos.[23]

Kui tribesmen anticipated a messenger who would bring their Lost Book back to the special places of worship built for such an anticipated event.[24] The **Lahu** also built 'Long Houses' for their awaited event which can still be found in their villages today.

The **Lisu** in Yunnan province, China, believe a King, one of their own would one day rule over them and restore their book in their language; even though the Lisu lack any form of writing and alphabet.[25]

---

[17] Don Richardson; *Eternity in their Hearts,* chapter two "Peoples of the Lost Book"; 3rd ed. 2005.

[18] Their name for a benign supernatural Being "whose shape and form exceeds man's ability to comprehend".

[19] Richardson, page 76

[20] Creator of all things

[21] Richardson page 77

[22] Ibid page 78

[23] Ibid page 79

[24] Ibid page 80

[25] Ibid

The **Naga** consist of twenty-four tribes and at least on tribe – *the Rengma*- remember *"the Supreme Being gave His words to their forefathers by writing them on animal skins. But the forefather did not take care of the skins. Dogs ate them up!"*[26] [27]

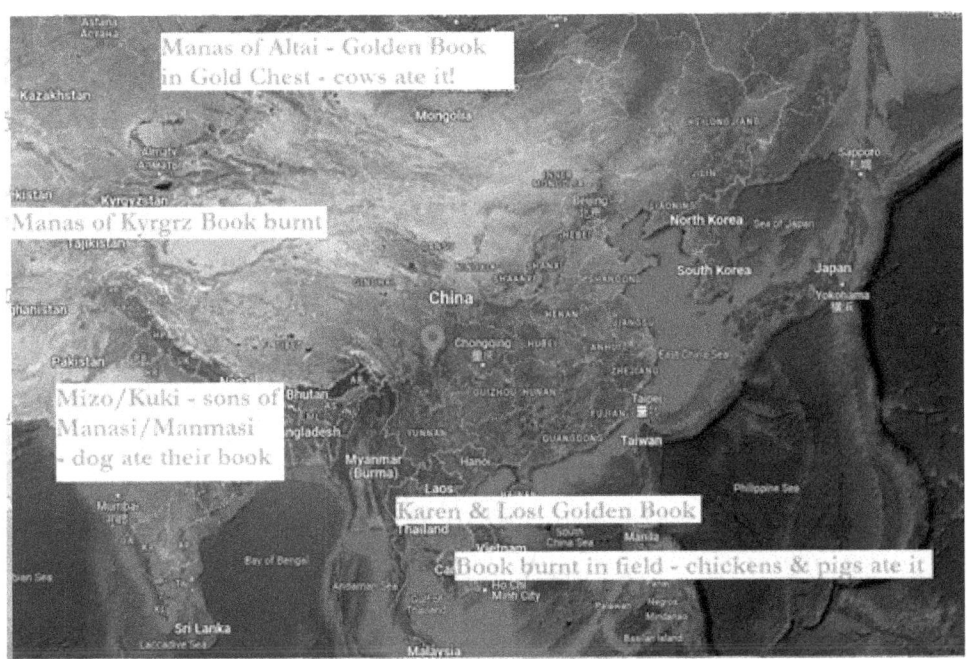

Different Israelite peoples around China 1 RED PIN is Xinlong, Gauze Prov. China

Mizo Israel identity researcher, Zaithanchhungi, writes *"According to the oral tradition of Mizo, the leather scrolls in which all ancestral history of the tribes and families were written, were lost due to continuous slavery. The leather Scrolls in which they had written about their origins, family histories and narratives of their travels were said to have been left behind in their labour camps when they fled China. According to another legend of the Mizo, the leather Scrolls were eaten by a dog of the keeper of the Scrolls."*

The **Mizo Kuki Chin** are sub-clans of the same people who connect the Hill Tribes of Myanmar not only back into China but back to Israel

---

[26] Ibid

[27] Tenegfeldt, *A Century of growth,* page 46

itself. Kuki ethnographer, Dr Khaplum M. Lenthang in his book documents his people as the people of Manmasi and writes;
Themthu and Lapi [poems and chants] ....*are reliable, sources concerning our origin and genealogy.*[28] He spent fifty years collecting these poems and chants and publishing them in books, both in English and Kuki, so that the history would be preserved – the very thing that the Lost Tribes Institute hopes to achieve. He goes on: *'These sources also prove that we once possessed the scroll but later lost it.'*[29]
Dr. Khuplam records volumes of these poems and chants this is one among many:

> *During the reign of Kutpi maangpa*
> *the Red-Sea had gone dried*
> *cloud in the day and fire in the night led the people*
> *many days and many nights together,*
> *like wild animals the water had swallowed*
> *we fetch water that originated from rock (stone)*
> *to satisfy the thirst of the people and their flock.*[30]

No doubt these people of "The Lost Book" are also people of "The Book". The story of the Israelites is unmistakable in the preceding Kuki poem. The Karen songs are also unmistaken as have come, also, from the 'Book'..

Kyrgyzstan and their Lost Book West of China across the Taklamakan Desert another people have a legend that confirms the legends of the Kuki Chin Mizo clans in northeast India; they are the Kyrgyz. Richard Hewitt writes "Sure enough Ashim Jakypbek's version Tengiri Manas, notes that Kitai leaders burned Kyrgyz scrolls:

---

[28] Dr Lenthang, *The Wonderful Genealogical Tales of Manmasi (Kuki-Chin-Mizo)* page 163

[29] Ibid

[30] Ibid Appendix II page i

When the Kitai, who say, "We are the only ones in this world who have knowledge," robbed the sacred fort and burned sacred writings from the treasury, they said, "May the darkness that has fallen on the Kyrgyz also come on their minds, so they might not know another writing."

Does the loss of this important book point to the reason for the Epics of the Kyrgyz and the poems and the stories of the Manmasi of northeast India? Dr Khuplam Milui Lenthang writes "Although the scroll was lost, the people evolved some games as in the old days. To some extent this helped to maintain continuity of the customs and culture."³¹

Altai and their Golden Book

North of the Kyrgyz, the Altai have a legend of a Golden Book just like the Karen.  The Altai Golden Book is also in a Golden Chest, reminiscent of the Golden Ark of biblical fame. In their version the golden chest falls in the water whilst crossing a river. They take the golden book out to dry the pages. A cow eats the pages and it is lost.³²

Don Richardson

Don Richardson, Christian anthropologist, who wrote the book, *Eternity in their hearts,* has a conundrum. Chapter 2, entitled *Peoples of the Lost Book,* documents the same people this paper is endeavouring to explain.

---

³¹ Dr Lenthang, The Wonderful Genealogical Tales of Manmasi (Kuki-Chin-Mizo) page 164

³² 31 BEDYUROV Brontoi Yangovich Chairman of Intl. Assoc. Of the Altaian Peoples IASAP, author and recipient of a Soviet award was bquoted saying on 28th June 2019 at WEF Scientific Symposium, Bishkek, Kyrgyzstan

For him, he says that the Karen people present a striking anomaly for the theologian.[33] They cannot have come in contact with Christians because there is no mention of an incarnation nor a Redeemer dying for man's sins and rising from the dead. Whilst having a clear awareness of basic scriptural facts, and the name of their God, Yu-wah, being eerily close to Yehovah, they lack the basics of the Jewish faith by not having any equivalents for Abraham and Moses. And how could they come into contact with Jewish thought, being 4000 miles from Jerusalem?, Richardson continues to write.

On page 75 he says, "Could it be that Karen beliefs about Yu-wah predate both Judaism and Christianity?" His answer is yes and Dr Francis Mason's is also "Yes". The form of Judaism we see today is often referred to as Rabbinic Judaism. This was formulated in 100AD at Yavneh and Rabbi Akiva was very instrumental in that process. Prior to that, there were twelve sects of Judaism (for want of a better word), in the Second Temple period. The scribes and Pharisees brought a very Deuteronomic form of religion back from the Babylonia captivity. The First Temple worship was dramatically different from Second Temple worship, according the Margaret Barker[34]. Also, the northern kingdom of Israel had broken away and started their own form of worship[35]. It is this latter group that both I and Dr Mason reckon the Karen traditions must have come from. In other words, they are a remnant of the Ten (lost) Tribes of the House of Israel. In Dr Mason's day [1834], this finding of the Karen as part of a much talked about mystery, had the appearance of incredibility, as Richardson says, "they are 4,000 miles from Jerusalem."

---

[33] Page 74 Eternity in their hearts by Don Richardson

[34] New thoughts on Temple Theology by Margaret Barker

[35] 2 Kings 12

McGowan and Israelites of Chengdu

However, within a couple of decades, Dr McGowan would be talking to the British Association in London about a colony of Jews [Israelites from the northern kingdom is clear from the context] in and around Chengdu in China that had existed there since the second century BC.

Torrance and the Ancient Israelites

Reverend Thomas T Torrance would find an Ancient Israelite people in the same place in 1920s. He writes extensively about them in his book, *China's First Missionaries:Ancient Israelites*[36]. Like the Karen they did not have Jewish understandings but they had clear biblical understandings. Here is a quote from Torrance's son:-

Bishop T.F. Torrance writes in his father book:

---

[36]Torrance 2nd edition 1988 page 8

"In 1925 I had the privilege of being present at the village of Oir, some ten thousand feet above sea level, situated in a lateral valley behind Weichou, when a venerable Chiang priest revealed to my father for the first time the full rite of the Day of Atonement in the Chiang liturgical year. When my father read to him the sixteenth chapter of the book of Leviticus, the priest leapt off his seat in excitement, exclaiming that these were the lost Chiang Scriptures." [37]

What Don Richardson overlooks is that the northern kingdom of Israel had been wandering in exile for over 2500[38] years and had indeed managed to make their way through the Silk Road of Central Asia, into China, and finally into the hills of Myanmar. An interesting side note to this is the Karen reckoning of years.

Karen Founding Year – BC 739

The Karen reckon 2010 to be their year 2749. This means that they look to BC 739 as the year of their founding. In their legends, Karen speak of coming from the land of 'Thibi Kawbi" which some have thought may indicate Tibet and the Gobi desert. Some Karen oral traditions refer to crossing a river of "running sand" as an important event in their history. There are Chinese sources which refer to the Gobi Desert as the "river of sand," and it is probable that the Karen originated in an area bordering Tibet. They crossed

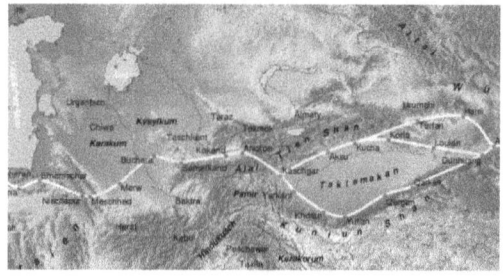

---

[37] Torrance 2nd Ed 1988 page vi

[38] 1830AD plus 740 years

the Gobi Desert into China, and gradually made their way into the mountainous areas of Burma. In ancient times most of Thailand's Karen came over the eastern borders of Burma, and this is still true today. The first Karen most likely immigrated to Thailand before the Thai, and just after the Mon Khmers. Today almost all of Thailand's Karen live in the western part of the country along the shared border with Burma.[39]

Are the Karen alone as Israelites?

So are there other Israelite peoples around today? Well indeed there are! This symposium[40], for which this paper is written, has the purpose of bringing together various researchers, whom have been labouring, for many decades - on their own - trying to get their findings out to a wider audience. Recently, we have found each other and our research findings (though not identical) rhyme with each other. A great example would be the Kyrgyz and the Japanese. Both have researchers claiming their peoples were once Ancient Israelites. The Kyrgyz have a story of two brothers – one ate meat and the other fish. They knew they were the meat eaters and that the Japanese were the fish eaters. Similarly, the Japanese have a story of two brothers - one ate meat and the other fish. They know they are the fish eaters but they don't know who or where their meat eating brother is.

We hope to form an institute[41] where many peoples may present their own research into a body of academics that can validate some or all of their findings. Sometimes assumptions made, especially among tribal peoples, need to be assessed alongside historical and scientific methodology. A "Lost Tribes Institute", like it has been proposed, can

---

[39] http://www.infomekong.com/peoples/karen/ Accessed 2014

[40] Lost Tribes Institute Symposium, Chiang Mai 9th & 10th May 2024

[41] This institute is being formed as of 20th May 2024

facilitate the publishing of those findings for the benefit of many, no less than the promises of God, to find the Lost Sheep of the House of Israel wherever they roamed, even to the ends of the earth.

Dr Howard Chung and Manchu of China

Dr Howard Chung, who is presenting at this Symposium, covers very well the Israelites in China.[42]

He has done extensive research on the waves of Israelites flowing into and out of China. This subject is too detailed to be given any justice here. I refer the reader to his book.

On page 373 he makes the claim that Manchu was not a place name, but rather a tribal name. They lived among the former Jachinites and Hebrews and therefore Manchu was a phonic rendition of an Israelite tribe – Manasseh comes to mind.

Yuezhis and Alans of Central Asia were referred to in Chinese literature as "Wen-na-sha". Considering the M-to-W phonetic shift brings us to the name Manasseh, he writes on page 117.

Richard Hewitt and the Manas Epic

It is the traditions in the Epic of Manas, which may hold the best connections of Manasseh to the N.E. India hill tribe peoples.

The Epic of Manas tells the story of Manas, his father Jayyb, his descendants, and their exploits against various foes, and in some versions the poem consists of approximately 500,000 lines.

---

[42] Dr Ha-Sung Chung, The History of Israelites in China Amazon.com 2023
https://www.academia.edu/83361421/
The_History_of_the_Israelites_in_China_from_1122_BC_to_1919_AD_%20As_documented_in_Manzhou_Yuanliu_Kao_%E6%BB%BF%E6%B4%B2%E6%BA%90%E6%B5%81%E8%80%83_

Richard Hewitt found over 300 Old testament stories or parallels in the Epic of Manas connecting the hero, Manas to the son of Joseph, Manasseh. Richard Hewitt lived among the Kyrgyz shepherds and in Kyrgyzstan for twenty years and has authored books and is also speaking at this symposium.

The Kyrgyz people are famous horsemen and they were known to travel thousands of kilometres to visit people they knew. There is the story of Jakyb's brother, from the other side of Tibet, coming to visit Jakyb. The famous Old Horse Tea Road show the trading routes connecting southern China to Tibet and Burma. Below is a map of the Manas National Park along the Manas River, bordering Bhutan and Assam, India. It seems the Kyrgyz left their name sake here.

Maps Including Kyrgyz & Qiang 600 BC [43]

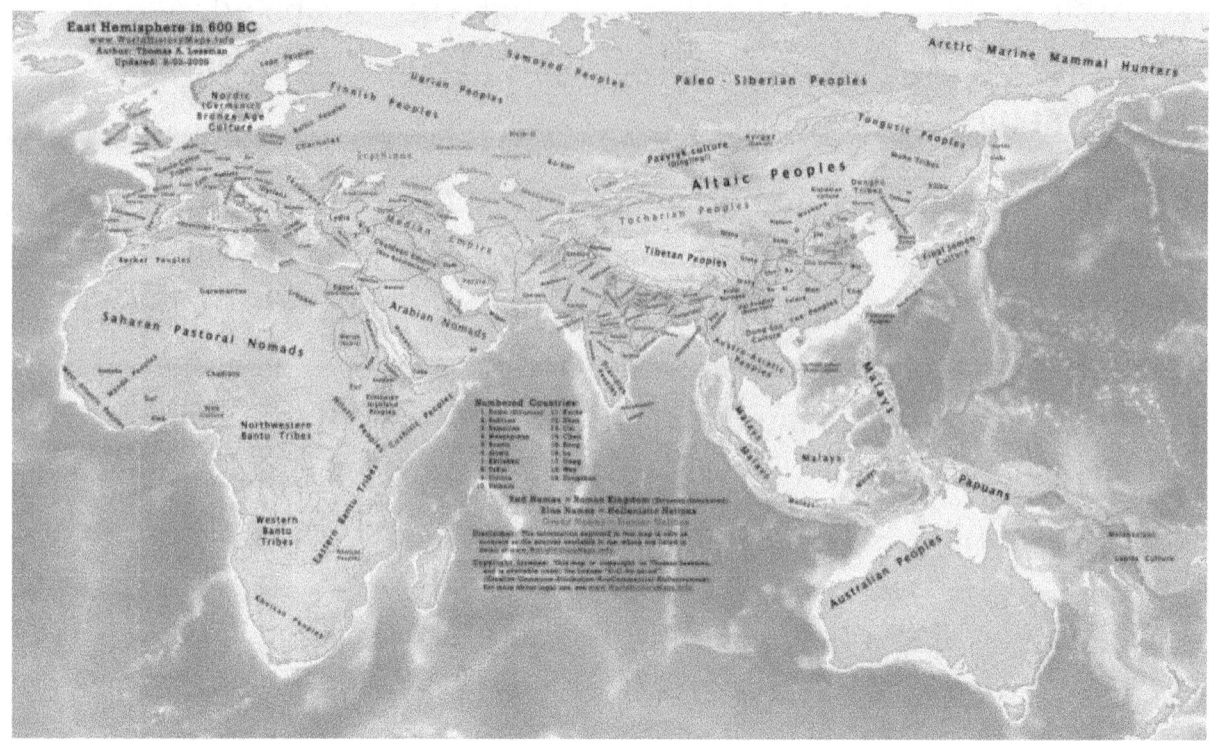

Kyrgyz, Altai and Qiang can be found in Central Asia, southern Siberia and western China, less than 200 years after the Assyrian captivity of the tribes of Israel.

Maps Horse Tea Trade Routes

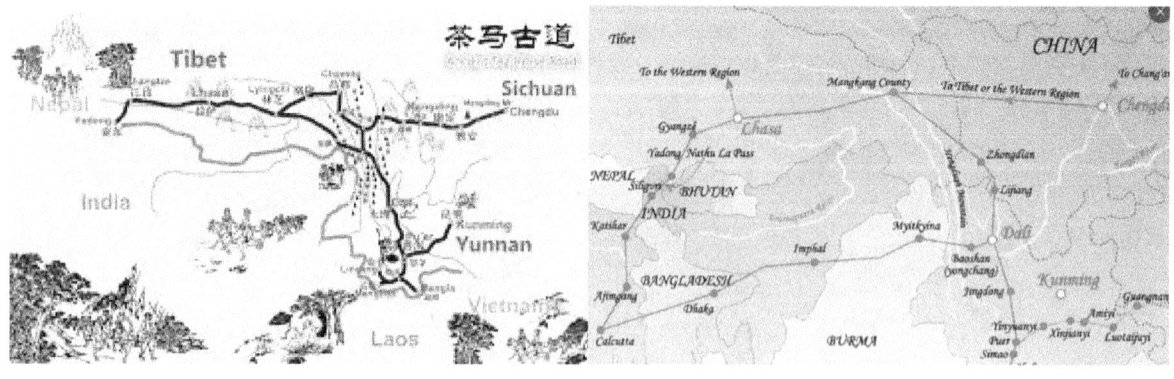

---

[43] https://www.worldhistorymaps.info/wp-content/uploads/2021/02/map-600bc.jpg

The horse tea route maps show the connections of Tibet with China and Myanmar (above) and between India and Central Asia (below).

The Kyrgyz as famous horsemen were no doubt involved in the Horse/Tea trade routes

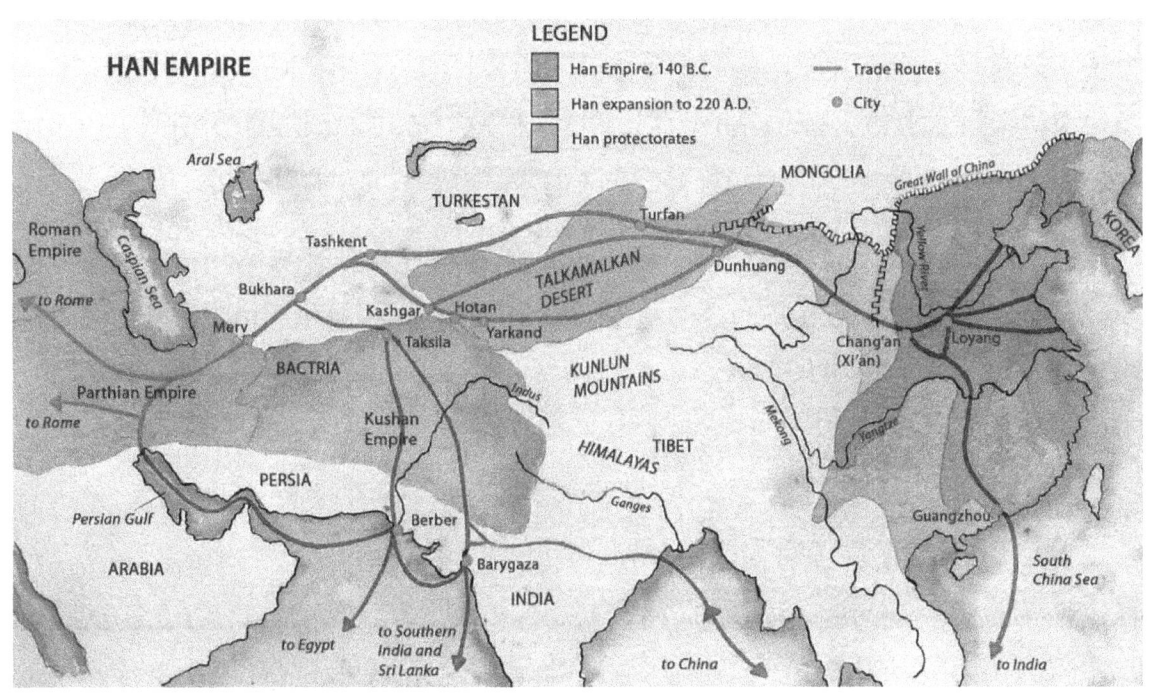

Kyrgyz - famous horsemen from 600 BC

Conclusion

Dr Mason appears, from his quotes of Karen *thah*, to see them expecting a heavenly city and a kingdom with their own king as the sole monarch.

References to a new town, a new city – a silver city[44], that Mason says equates with the establishment of the *mountain heights* reminds us of what the writer in Hebrews says of Abraham in chapter 11;

---

[44] Page 217 May 1834 Mason Calcutta Christian Observer

> *9 By faith he dwelt in the promised land as a stranger in a foreign country. He lived in tents, as did Isaac and Jacob, who were heirs with him of the same promise. 10 For he was looking forward to the city with foundations, whose architect and builder is God.*

When the missionaries found them, in the 1800s, the Karen were already living in the faith of Abraham. They were expecting a coming kingdom and a king.

Perhaps this kingdom message should be revisited. Restoring age-old foundations, which is an end of age expectation, could be the means of restoring Karen culture.

Isaiah 58:11 The LORD will always guide you; He will satisfy you in a sun-scorched land and strengthen your frame. You will be like a well-watered garden, like a spring whose waters never fail. 12 Your people will rebuild the ancient ruins; you will restore the age-old foundations; you will be called Repairer of the Breach, Restorer of the Streets of Dwelling.

Isaiah 61:4 says *"They will rebuild the ancient ruins; they will restore the places long devastated; they will renew the ruined cities, the desolations of many generations."*

The Karen, as having left the land of their ancestors, in 739 BC, continued to expect a return of a kingdom and a kingdom age and a divine heavenly appointed – David-like - king.

This understanding of Yu-wah, the Karen God, must be informed from the first temple worship of Yehovah; for they went into captivity between the era of the two temples. Worshipping at the high places in groves was the norm for the northern kingdom of Israel during this period. Looking back to the Tabernacle of David must also be a memory that they kept alive – their Great Doo who played the harp.

The Q'iang Min of Torrance's time (1920s) worshipped in groves on the high places. That the Karen came from these people seems to fit the facts, although it is many, many centuries ago.

Regardless, the Karen, from the evidence presented here are from the Ten Tribes of Israel – having wandered through many exiles and migrations – they kept their hope alive of the return of their king through songs and the worship of their God, Yu-wah. They held a strong expectation of a kingdom age where everyone will be happy.

Bibliography

1. Allen, J.H., *Judah's Scepter and Joseph's Birthright*, Originally published, 1902. Nineteenth Edition. Re-typeset, A.D. 2000
2. Avichail, R. Eliyahu., *The Tribes of Israel* 5765 Amishav Jerusalem
3. Barker, Margaret,. *Temple Theology – An Introduction* 23rd April 2004 SPCK Publishing
4. Chen, Esther., *The Hidden Q'iang – Sons of Sheep* Abridged edition English
5. Chung, Ha-Sang Howard *Dispersion of the Israelites in the Eurasian Continent: How GOD has fulfilled His Promise: History of Eurasia from Biblical Perspective* Amazon Paperback – July 27, 2023
6. Collins, Steven M., *Israel's Lost Empires* 2004 Bible Blessings Royal Oak M.I.
7. Collins, Steven M., *Parthia The forgotten Ancient Superpower and its role in Biblical History* 2004 Bible Blessings Royal Oak M.I.
5. Drummond Joseph F, *2300 Days of Hell* 2014 Xlibris Corporation,
6. Gawler, Col.J.C., *Our Scythian Ancestors Identified with Israel*
7. Grant, Asahel; *The Nestorians or the Lost Tribes* John Murray, London 1841
8. Halkin, Hillel. *Across the Sabbath River* 2002 Houghton Mifflin Company New York
8. Lendering, Jona *Alexander the Great The Demise of the Persian Empire,* [340-320BC] 2004 Athenaeum Polak & Van Gennep Amsterdam
9. Lenthang, Dr Khuplam Milui. *The Wonderful Tales of the Manmasi (Kuki-Chin-Mizo)* 2013 Maxford Books Delhi.
10. Mallory, J.P. & Mair, Victor H. *The Tarim Mummies: Ancient China and the Mystery of the Earliest Peoples from the West* Thames & Hudson, 2000 - Social Science – 352 pages
11. Moore, George M.D. *The Lost Tribes and the Saxons of the East and of the West: With new views of Buddhism, and translations of rock-records in India* 1861 London, Longmans, Green, Longman, and Roberts
12. Moore, Thomas *History of Ireland* 1843 Lea & Blanchard, Philadelphia

13. Rice, Tamara Talbot, *The Scythians* 3rd edition 1961 F.A. Praeger;
14. Richardson, Don *Eternity in their hearts* 3rd Ed. 2005 Regal Books. Ventura, California
15. Risbek (Hewitt, Richard) *Manas - Lost & Found: A Bridge Linking Kyrgyzstan's Epic toAncient Oracles* 2012 Risbek California
16. Richard Hewitt et al. *The Interconnectedness of the Israelites in Asia: Lost Tribes Institute's First Scientific Symposium* by Richard Hewitt (Author), Margot Crossing (Author), Arimasa Kubo (Author), Kengo Nagami (Author), & 6 more Published on Amazon Dec 2023
17. Shachan, Dr Avigdor, *In the Footsteps of the Ten Lost Tribes* 2007 CreateSpace Translated from the Hebrew 2003 version *Towards the Sambatyon River - a Journey in the Footsteps of the Ten Tribes* Hakibbutz Hameuchad Pub. House, Tel Aviv
18. Shu-min Huang & Cheng-kuang Hsu *Imaging China: Regional Division and National Unity* Ed.Taipei: Institute of Ethnology. http://ultra.ihp.sinica.edu.tw/~origins/pages/barbarbook4.htm Accessed 15/4/16
19. Spykermann, Stephen J. *A Game changing revelation:The Hidden Ancestry of America & Great Britain* September 2014 Legends Library Publishing NY
20. Torrance, Rev. Thomas T., *China's First Missionaries: Ancient 'Israelites '* 2nd Edition 1988 Daniel Shaw Co. Chicago.
21. 18. Zaithanchhungi, *Israel-Mizo Identity* 2008 Hope Lodge, Aizawl

Websites accessed
http://www.biblesearchers.com/hebrewchurch/primitive/losttribesisrael10.shtml Retrieved 28/4/16
https://www.geni.com/projects/Where-are-The-Ten-Lost-Tribes-of-Israel/3474 Retrieved 20/4/2016
https://sovereignwales.com/tag/khumric-welsh/ Retrieved 28/4/16
http://ultra.ihp.sinica.edu.tw/~origins/pages/barbarbook4.htm Accessed 15/4/16

Academia.edu Researchers
Prof (Dr) WA Liebenberg @ academia.edu
https://hrti.academia.edu/ProfDrWALiebenberg?swp=tc-au-30701941
Richard (Risbek) Hewitt @ academia.edu
https://losttribesinstitute.academia.edu/RichardRisbekHewitt
https://arabaev.academia.edu/RichardHewitt?swp=tc-au-118343285
Howard Ha-Sang Chung @ academia.edu
https://handong.academia.edu/HaSungChung?swp=tc-au-83361421
Margot Crossing @ academia.edu
https://losttribesinstitute.academia.edu/MargotCROSSING

Videos
https://www.youtube.com/@losttribescafe7966 Lost Tribes Café Youtube Channel
https://rumble.com/user/LostTribesFound Lost Tribes Found Rumble Channel
https://www.youtube.com/watch?v=y_hPnIWf_h0 Martin Trench Lost Tribes of Israel
Dr Avigdor Sharchan interview https://www.youtube.com/watch?v=IZBoEjRxiek JAPAN AND THE 10 LOST TRIBES OF ISRAEL
Arimasa Kubo interview https://www.youtube.com/watch?v=RrXtrHwynrY The Shinto Religion and Judaism i24NEWS English
https://www.youtube.com/@myjewishjapan My Jewish Japan channel

https://www.youtube.com/channel/UC0jKKZxOwVzFLvQJIyrwvuA Mikkel S Kragh Channel

Websites and blogs
Arimasa Kubo https://remnant-p.com/engindex.htm
Margot Crossing https://losttribesfoundblog.wordpress.com/
Steven M Collins https://stevenmcollins.com/ eBook available
Margaret Barker: Temple Theology http://www.margaretbarker.com/Temple/default.htm
Mikkel S Kragh https://www.nordiskisrael.dk/
Robert Mock M.D. http://www.biblesearchers.com/

Esther Chen; The Hidden Q'iang - Sons of Sheep

https://www.dropbox.com/scl/fi/769mf0jeslaoueimfwh7f/Abridged-Version-1.pdf?rlkey=7h9q32bda5viscehhsegbm49j&dl=0

Rev Thomas T Torrance; China's First Missionaries: Ancient Israelite https://www.dropbox.com/scl/fo/1qgko94ny9m2odya2kp3e/h?rlkey=utsshtpyn0jb0m5o0ib9zt2rv&dl=0

Karen of Burmah – A remnant of the Ten Tribes of Israel May 1834 by Dr Fancis Mason

Karen of Burmah - A Remnant of the Ten Tribes of Israel; 1835 Dr Fancis Mason

Contact
Lost Tribes Institute

Margot Crossing https://losttribesinstitute.academia.edu/MargotCROSSING
Richard Hewitt https://losttribesinstitute.academia.edu/RichardRisbekHewitt
Howard Ha-Sang Chung https://handong.academia.edu/HaSungChung?swp=rr-ac-83361421

Video Message From Central Asia to Southeast Asia By Damir Eraliev
Chiang Mai, Thailand Symposium May 9th, 2024

My name is Damir Eraliev. I'm Kyrgyz.

Ethnic Kyrgyz pass scriptural truths from generation to generation within their oral epic "Manas" and within their ancient customs and traditions.

When did the Kyrgyz have the "*Sudur Bichik*" (Sacred Scripture)? According to different opinions, the enemies of Kyrgyz destroyed the sacred book. Some say the holy writings were burned by the Chinese. Others say it sank to the bottom of the sea. Even without the book, many observe that Kyrgyz obey the customs and traditions of the Good Book more than Jews and Christians. The Torah and Gospel seem to be woven into Kyrgyz culture.

Where did the Kyrgyz get the book? The poet Togolok Moldo said that the Sayak tribe, a large Kyrgyz tribe, settled on the banks of the Nile. Public activist historian and researcher Dastan Sarygulov compares the Kyrgyz to the Sumerian civilization, in other words, he notes that Kyrgyz were part of the Sumerian culture. Abraham was in Sumeria and Egypt. Moses and Israel's twelve tribes were also in Egypt.

The scientist Shabalov Alexander Sakratovich says that the Kyrgyz appeared in Central Asia in the III-II centuries BC. As shown in the work "O Kyrgyzakh": Kyrgyz are one of the oldest nations. According to the Chronicle Tanshu, Kyrgyz first appeared in Eastern Turkestan, Semierechye or "Seven Rivers", and the present territory of Kyrgyzstan in the 2nd-3rd centuries AD, where their language gradually spread to the surrounding tribes and peoples -to Dulatov, Usunei, Sakov, Uighur, Tokhar, and other nationalities.

What can we say based on this information? The Kyrgyz ancestors existed in the area from the third century BC, or at the latest, the second century AD.
In the Manas Epic, a national legend that preserves many customs from the Torah, it is written that one Kyrgyz named Uson, one of the ten elders of Orozdu, was expelled to Indystan (India) by the Chinese Khan, Alooke.

The epilogue of the epic storyteller Sayakbaya includes the widespread belief that the epic characters Semetey, Bakay, Kanykei, Kul-choro and Aichurek did not die and did not simply disappear, but fled to distant India. Russian scientist V. M. Zhirmudskyi, also wrote that the heroes of the Manas Epic settled in distant India. V. M. Zhirmundsky, believes the lost heroes generate messianic ideas about the return of their hero Semetey, who will restore the golden age and national prosperity."

India still has ethnic groups who consider themselves Kyrgyz, or descendants of Manas or Orozdu.

The evil Alooke exiled Orozdu's two sons, Uson and Kyzylbek to go beyond the Kangai Mountain to the depths of China and Manchuria, and now they live in a dark forest that cannot be crossed in forty days. (The Kyrgyz call it Southeast Asia.) Our epic says it is a jungle. If we pay attention to the story, we see that Uson and Kyzylbek represent Southeast Asia. According to our beliefs in Kyrgyzstan, they have lost their language and their heart to the locals.

If we look at the map of the Great Silk Road, we can see the migration of many peoples. The trail is from Crimea's Sea of Azov to Japan. If our customs and traditions are similar to yours, then we know why. We are ancient kin.

Kyzylbek can be understood as "Redskin." Native American tribes are still called red to this day.... Why? Also, the Karen, like us, have evidence they are from the Lost Tribes of Israel and also have a tribe called the Red Karens.

We read that Uson, one of the ten sons of Orozdu, reached China beyond Kangai, grew up in the hands of Kozkaman and Kokchokoz (Blue Eyes), and gave his heart to China-Manchu forever.

The American researcher Mr. Richard Hewitt points out that ethnic groups in northeast India such as Assam, Mizoram, and Kuki identified themselves as Benei Manashe (descendants of biblical Manase). I confidently agree with Richard Hewitt that these ethnic groups, who even today live in these areas and consider themselves as descendants of Manas/Menashe……. I can confidently emphasize that Mizo, Assamese, and Kuki are related to me and my Kyrgyz people. If you read the Manas Epic, you are reading ancient portions of the Torah (sacred book), our lost Sudur Bichik. My people may have lost the physical copy but they kept it in their minds and passed it on to their descendants in the form of our oral epics for many generations to this day, since about 1800 BC.

I emphasize that Manas and Manasseh are the same person. One is mentioned in our oral epic, and the other is written in the Torah.

I strongly believe that your people and my people will continue this research together and strengthen God's bonds of brotherly love across Asia!!! In unity, we will put the Creator's fascinating puzzle together.

Israelites Who Migrated to Ancient Japan by Arimasa Kubo

I am honored to speak at this symposium. Today I would like to speak about the Lost Tribes of Israel who migrated to ancient Japan.

Previously, I had the privilege of guiding late Rabbi Eliyahu Avichail who visited Japan. He investigate d the Israelite remnants who migrated to ancient Japan. The Rabbi often spoke about the Shinlung tribe, located in Myanmar and northern India.

More recently, Professor Hidemichi Tanaka of Tohoku University has highlighted the substantial migration of the Israelite diaspora to ancient Japan.

The photos are clay statues of ancient Japanese men unearthed from tombs dating back to the third or fourth century CE. Observably, these figures exhibit a hairstyle reminiscent of the Israelite tradition, known as peyot or sidelocks, as prescribed in Leviticus 19:27 of the Bible: "You shall not shave around the sides of your head, nor shall you disfigure the edges of your beard." The presence of this distinct combination of peyot, long beards, and headwear suggests a significant population of Israelites in ancient Japan.

During the third or fourth century CE, coinciding with the arrival of the renowned Hata clan, ancient Japan witnessed a significant influx of immigrants. I think that these clay statues represent the appearance of individuals of the Hata clan. Many researchers believe that the Hata people were ancient Israelites.

However, the Hata clan was not the initial Israelite group to settle in Japan. Prior to their arrival, there were multiple waves of Israelite immigrants. The earliest wave likely occurred during BCE times. These early settlers introduced the Shinto religion to Japan. Shinto, meaning "the Way of God," serves as the traditional national religion of Japan and bears striking similarities to the ancient Israeli Way of God.

Both traditions emphasize the importance of purity and the rejection of impurity, eschew idol worship, and feature architectural resemblances between Shinto shrines and the Tabernacle of Moses. Moreover, Japanese customs often parallel those of ancient Israel, further suggesting a historical connection between the two cultures.

It's fascinating how the research unveils the intricate connections between ancient Israelites and the development of Shinto in Japan. It seems that multiple waves of Israelite migrants traversed through China and the Korean peninsula before reaching Japan.

The Israelites who arrived in Japan during BCE times likely laid the foundation for Shinto, instilling it as a fundamental aspect of Japanese spirituality. Then, during the third or fourth century CE, the arrival of the Hata people, another group of Israelites, further enriched and expanded the practice of Shinto across Japan, establishing it as the prevailing teaching for the Japanese people.

My study suggests that the Israelite diaspora faced persecution in China, leading to their dispersion into various groups. Some ventured eastward, eventually reaching Japan, while others journeyed southward, settling in mountainous regions near Tibet, giving rise to tribes such as the Chiang-Min, Shinlung, Mizos and Karen.

The parallels between the Japanese Mikoshi and the ancient Israelite Ark of the Covenant are striking. Both serve as portable sanctuaries, symbolizing the presence of the divine wherever they are carried. The Mikoshi, adorned with the legendary celestial bird Ho-oh, reflects the union of male and female symbolism, much like the cherubim atop the Ark of Israel.

During the procession of the Mikoshi, the chant "Essa" resonates, a term that, interestingly, translates to "lift up" in Hebrew, evoking a sense of reverence and elevation akin to the spiritual significance associated with the Ark. Furthermore, the phrase "En yara yah," although its exact meaning might elude understanding for many, bears resemblance to the Hebrew expression "Ani ahalel yah," signifying "I praise Yah.".

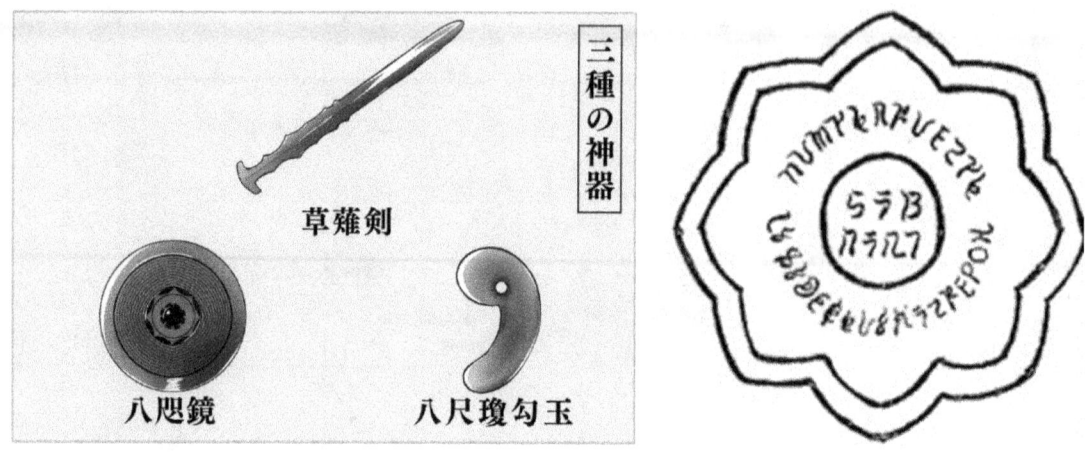

The sacred treasures of the Japanese imperial succession, comprising a mirror, a sword, and a bead, have been revered since the time of the first emperor. Kept away from public view, these artifacts hold immense significance in Japanese culture. While the mirror is rarely seen by outsiders, there are claims that it bears inscriptions resembling Hebrew words. Speculations suggest that these inscriptions could be interpreted as "I AM (asher eheyeh)" or "Light of Yahweh (or yhwh)." Additionally, the bead, shaped like the Hebrew letter yod (?), resembles the pronunciation "Yah," a shortened form of Yahweh.

Ise-jingu, situated in Ise City, Mie, Japan, holds a revered status as the foremost Shinto shrine. Throughout its history, it underwent several relocations within the Kinki area, Japan, before finding its permanent home in Ise. Despite settling in Ise, the shrine maintains a tradition of periodic reconstruction and temporary relocation to neighboring lands every twenty years.

This practice echoes the mobility of the tabernacle in ancient Israel, which accompanied the Israelites during their journey through the desert following their exodus from Egypt. Both the tabernacle and Ise-jingu are constructed primarily from wood, and the simple architectural design of Ise-jingu shares numerous similarities with the tabernacle.

The parallels between the structures and rituals of Ise-jingu and ancient Israelite practices are indeed fascinating. According to the Jewish Encyclopedia, the entrance to the Holy of Holies in the Jerusalem temple featured twelve steps, mirroring the entrance to the Holy of Holies in Ise-jingu, which also has twelve steps. Additionally, just as there was a curtain separating the Holy of Holies from the Holy Place in the Israeli tabernacle, a similar curtain exists between the Holy of Holies and the area for prayer at Ise-jingu.

These shared elements in structure and ritual deepen our understanding of potential cultural and historical connections between these distinct traditions. The attire worn by the priests of Ise-jingu further reinforces these parallels, as they don white robes adorned with hats, waistbands, tzitzit-like fringes, and ephod-like cloth, resembling the attire of the Levite priests who served in the tabernacle of Israel.

The legend surrounding the origins of Kono Shrine, one of the originals of Ise-jingu during its relocation, is both captivating and steeped in myth. According to this legend, in ancient times, a ladder connected heaven and earth, serving as a pathway for gods to ascend and descend. Kono Shrine was then erected as the abode of these divine beings. Eventually, the ladder collapsed, giving rise to the Ama-no-hashidate sandbar in the sea, celebrated for its breathtaking scenery.

This tale bears a striking resemblance to the biblical narrative in which Jacob, in a dream, beheld a ladder extending between heaven and earth, with angels ascending and descending upon it. Jacob, upon awakening, deemed the place as the House of God.

The parallels between the story of Abraham and Isaac and a Shinto festival at Suwa-taisha in Japan are intriguing. Situated at the base of a mountain named Moriya, reminiscent of the Temple Mount in Jerusalem, Suwa-taisha holds significance in the context of the Abraham and Isaac narrative.

Approximately 4000 years ago, Abraham journeyed with his son Isaac to the land of Moriyah, where he intended to offer him as a sacrifice. At Suwa-taisha, there stands a building known as Jukkenro, which bears a striking resemblance to the tabernacle of ancient Israel. Within the Holy of Holies of Jukkenro, during the festival on April 15th, the Mikoshi ark is placed on the western side, mirroring the arrangement of the Israeli tabernacle.

The similarities extend beyond mere architectural resemblance; the Jukkenro house aligns with the Israeli tabernacle in terms of size, orientation, construction, and purpose. The ritual enacted at Jukkenro, where a boy is bound to a pillar and threatened with a knife before being freed, bears a striking resemblance to the biblical story of Isaac's near-sacrifice by his father Abraham. In both narratives, a boy is bound with a rope and placed in a sacrificial position, only to be spared at the last moment by divine intervention.

In the Jukkenro ritual, as in the biblical story, the act of lowering the knife symbolizes the imminent sacrifice, but intervention prevents harm, and the boy becomes a symbol of blessings for the community. This tradition is annually commemorated at Suwa-taisha in a simplified form known as Ontohsai or the Misakuchi festival, echoing the story of Isaac's ordeal.

It's noteworthy that the term "Misakuchi" is believed to have its origins in Hebrew, specifically from the words "Mi-Itzhak-tin," meaning "from the story of Isaac."

The parallels between the story of Abraham and Isaac and the Misakuchi festival at Suwa-taisha continue with the sacrificial aspect. In the biblical narrative, after Isaac's release, Abraham discovers a ram caught in a thicket and offers it as a sacrifice in place of his son, referring to it as the provision of God. Similarly, until 1871, during the Misakuchi festival, deer were sacrificed at Suwa-taisha.

Due to the absence of sheep in ancient Japan, deer, a kosher animal, were utilized instead. Among the sacrificial deer, one with a split ear was particularly revered, believed to be the one provided by God. This deer's significance resonates with the biblical account of the ram caught in the thicket. It's plausible that like the deer, the ram sacrificed by Abraham may have had a split ear due to its entanglement.

The faith and cultural practices observed in these regions likely stem from the influx of Israelites who immigrated to Japan during ancient times, possibly during the BCE era. Additionally, the Hata people arrived in Japan in the third or fourth century CE, developed the Shinto faith, and built many Shinto shrines all over Japan.

Many researchers speculate that the Hata people were not only of Israelite descent but also Eastern Christians. This theory suggests that there were Israelites who had converted to Eastern Christianity, potentially during their time in Central Asia, where Christianity had gained traction as early as the second century CE. The Hata people exhibited both Israeli and Christian characteristics, including their belief in the Trinity. The photo is a tripod built by the Hata people, symbolizing their faith in the Trinity of God.

The connection between the Hata people and the spread of INARI Shinto shrines across Japan is indeed intriguing. The theory proposes that "INARI" originated from "INRI," the title placed above Jesus' head on the cross, meaning Jesus of Nazareth, King of the Jews.

Due to the absence of the letter "N" in the ancient Japanese language, the Hata clan adapted "Na," the first two characters of Nazareth, to represent the sound in "INARI."

Furthermore, the layout of Heian-kyo, the capital of Japan built by the Hata people in the 8th century CE in today's Kyoto, featured streets arranged in a grid pattern resembling a T-shaped cross. The grid pattern consists of rectangle and square districts. If you see only rectangle districts, you will see a T-shaped cross, on which Jesus was crucified.

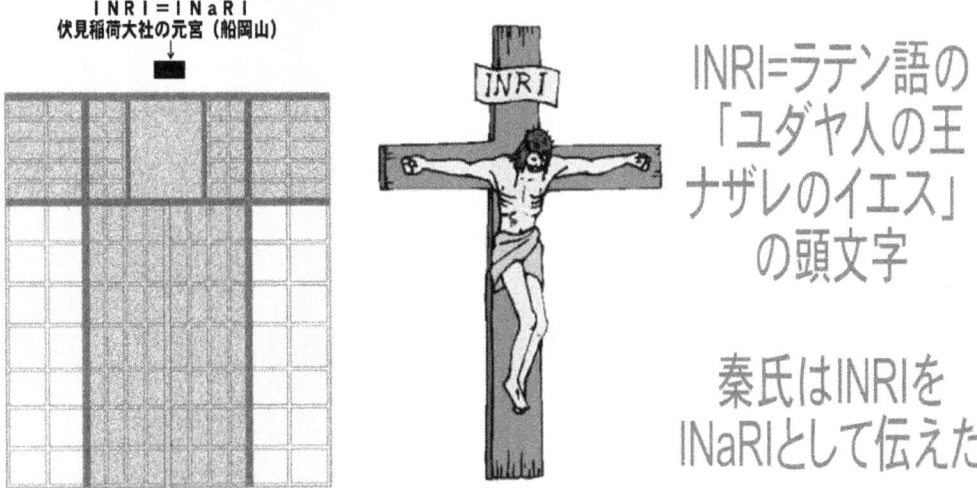

The emperor's palace occupied the location corresponding to Jesus' head, while Mt. Funaoka represented the site of the accusation plate. The original INaRI shrine, located atop Mt. Funaoka, aligns with the place of Jesus' cross, further reinforcing the connection between INARI shrines and the Hata clan's Christianity.

Ancient Japan was thus founded and developed by the Israelite diaspora and ancient Israelite Eastern Christians. So, I believe all the Japanese must come back to the faith in Biblical God Yahweh and His Savior Jesus Christ (Yeshua HaMashiah) since our ancestors had believed in Biblical God. All the descendants of ancient Israelites in Asia and the world must come back to the faith in God of the Bible.

Hata Clan by Dr. Kengo Nagami

The Hata Clan had an enormous influence on ancient Japanese society. They used to live in the Yuzuki Kingdom in Central Asia (the western part of Xinjiang, Uyghur Autonomous Region today). Ethnically, they were ancient Israelites; whether they were descendants of the Northern Kingdom of Israel or the Southern Kingdom of Judah is still undecided.

The members of the Hata clan became Christian, because ancient Eastern Christianity, searching for Israel's lost tribes, had already reached a large part of Central Asia by the end of the 2nd century. Missionaries were active there. For instance, the Apostle Thomas went to Armenia and then to India to proclaim the Good News. Since ancient Eastern Christianity preserved Jewish influences, the people of the Hata Clan became Christian without any difficulties.

According to "Nihon Shoki," the Chronicles of Japan, the King of Yuzuki came from China at the end of the 3rd century with approximately 25,000 people, and they were the Hata Clan. Before coming to Japan, they wandered in the Asian Continent for a long time and finally settled in ancient China. They served the first Qin Emperor and many members of the Hata Clan became officials of the Qin Dynasty since they had enormous wealth and tremendous technology for civil engineering and construction. After the Qin Dynasty's fall, the Hata clan moved to the Korean Peninsula and finally came to Japan at the end of the 3rd century. Interestingly, the Chinese character for Qin and Hata are the same. Hata is a Japanese reading of Qin.

The Hata clan settled in Uzumasa

After settling in Uzumasa in Kyoto, the Hata Clan's population increased. In the 5th century, in the era of Emperor Yuryaku, there were 18,670 people in 92 offices. In the 6th century, there were at least 7,053 houses, or about 20,000~30,000 Hata people.

The town's name, Uzumasa, is interesting. The Chinese characters for it are "thick" and "Hata". Its reading, Uzumasa, has nothing to do with the Chinese characters and originally means "Ishu Masha" in Aramaic, meaning Jesus the Messiah.

The technology and culture that the Hata people brought were highly sophisticated. They built irrigation canals, many wooden architectural structures that are seen in Shinto shrines and Buddhist temples, and large ancient tombs (Kofun). During the 6th Century Asuka era, the Hata clans also introduced silkworm culture, weaving technology, and sake brewing.

Kawakatsu Hata and Prince Shotoku

Politically and economically speaking, the influence of the Hata clan was enormous. Kawakatsu Hata was highly active as a member of Prince Shotoku's council. Utilizing tremendous wealth and construction technology, Kawakatsu Hata and his team built the Heian-kyo Central Palace for the emperor in ancient Kyoto.

As a follower of UzaMasa (Messiah Jesus), Kawakatsu Hata influenced the emperor's family, especially Prince Shotoku's mother. She became a follower of Jesus and named her son "Umayato-no-Miko," i.e., "Prince of the stable door" - that was Prince Shotoku's childhood name. His mother wanted her son to be like Jesus who was born in a stable and considered the true door or gate to the sheep's stable or coral.

Christian influence in Shinto: Yahata shrine and Inari shrine

Kawakatsu Hata and his clan members also built many Shinto shrines, which were called Yahata (or Hachiman) shrine and the Inari shrine. The word, Yahata consists of two parts: 1) Ya which is Yahweh, and 2) Hata the clan's name. So, Yahata means "God of Hata."

The name, Inari, is also interesting. Inari seems to come from "INRI," the shortened form of Jesus' crime bill which stated "Iesus Nazarenus Rex Iudaeorum" and hung on the top of the cross. Therefore, Inari shrines are said to be Jesus' shrines. About 80% of Shinto shrines are believed to be Yahata shrines and Inari shrines.

In Uzumasa, there is "Kaiko-no-Yashiro" (silkworm shrine) which historians say Kawakatsu Hata built. Interestingly, that shrine has a "three pillar torii." Usually, "torii" is one single entrance gate with two side poles. If you look at this "three pillar torii" from above, it is a beautiful triangle. That symbolizes the Divine Trinity. The Hata clan's Christian influence can be seen in the foundation of Shintoism even today.

Christian influence in Buddhism

Kawakatsu Hata also built Koryu-ji temple in 603, which was later called "Uzumzsa (Jesus the Messiah) temple", named after the Hata clan's hometown. At that time, at the end of the 6th century, Nestorian Christianity also reached Japan, and its influence along with the Hata Clan's existence became enormous on Japanese Buddhism.

However, Japanese Buddhism followed the original belief of Hinayana (or Theravada which means "small vehicle") Buddhism, which emphasized "self-reliance" for a long time. In the 9th century, Monk Kuukai studied Buddhism in China, which was influenced by Nestorian Christianity, and started a new Shingon sect which means "True Word" like the Logos Christ in John's Gospel.

In the late 12th and early 13th century, Japanese Buddhism changed. Honen started a new sect of Jodo-shu, and his disciple Shinran started Jodo-sinshu. Both emphasized "salvation by faith in Amidabutsu". In other words, "relying on someone else" is called Mahayana Buddhism. In its teaching, Amidabutsu (Amida Buddha) is like a savior who saves people from sins. People can't save themselves. Human duty is only trusting in Amidabutsu by chanting Nembutsu, "Namu Amidabutsu," which means to believe in Amidabutsu. Interestingly, Amidabutsu has two names, Amitabha and Amitayu. Amitabha means "eternal light," and Amitayu means "eternal life." It is so obvious that these eternal elements are just like those of Jesus, who is known as eternal light and has eternal life (1 John 1:1~7). Amidabutsu is a Buddhist version of Christ.

Similarities between Japanese and Israelites: New Year tradition

Finally, I want to add some interesting comments about the Japanese New Year celebration. Those elements are deeply influenced by the Exodus event in the Old Testament. First, we Japanese clean up the entire house before the New Year. That tradition is remarkably similar to the ancient Israelites' tradition of Passover and eating unleavened bread. The Israelites were told to clean up the house so it is without any leaven. The Lord told Moses to remember the day of Passover as the New Year and to keep this ritual every year (Exodus 12).

Secondly, we Japanese eat Mochi (rice cake) on the New Year's Day, and that is like Israel's Matzah (unleavened bread) eaten at the Passover dinner. Mochi and Matzah interestingly sound similar.

Thirdly, we Japanese drink a cup of sake on the New Year Day morning, which is called "Toso." The Chinese character for "To" means to slaughter, and that for "So" means to revive. This is Death and Resurrection! Drinking "Toso" symbolizes the Good News that Jesus died for us as the Passover Lamb and was resurrected to give us eternal life.

I believe that those New Year traditions surely came from Hebraic culture and belief and that the ancient Israelites, both the remnant of the lost ten tribes and that of the tribe of Judah, brought them to Japan via the Silk Road before the Hata clan came.

Israelite Migrations Across Asia (Korea & SE Asia) by Howard Ha-Sung Chung

History of the Koreans and their Descendants

Told following Psalm 107

Content

1. In the end times, Lord Jehovah will gather the scattered Israelites from all over the world.

2. They were scattered because they rebelled against their God: They were enslaved

3. They came to China by Sea.

3.1 Levirat

3.2 The Asylum Cities

3.3 Sukkot: The Feast of Tabernacles (Leviticus 23:34).

3.4 The name Chaoxian: Shoshan

> They became great for God blessed them.
> They were destroyed again and again

1. In the end times, Lord Jehovah will gather the scattered Israelites from all over the world

1 O give thanks unto the LORD, for he is good: for his mercy endureth forever. 2 Let the redeemed of the LORD say so, whom he hath redeemed from the hand of the enemy; 3 And gathered them out of the lands, from the east, and from the west, from the north, and from the south.

Korea, like the Karen people in the second half of the 19th century, adopted Christianity because they recognized Christianity as the religion of their ancestors. The history of Christianity in Korea is strange because it has largely occurred without Western missionaries.

The evangelization of Korea began 250 years before the first arrival of a Western missionary. This, too, is a wondrous story that can only be explained by accounting the Israeli background of the Koreans: They remembered their Ancient God through the Bible.

In 1583, Matteo Ricci, an Italian Jesuit, entered China to establish the Chinese Jesuit Mission. In 1602 he wrote a tract entitled The True Meaning of the Lord of Heaven (天主實義, Tianzhu Shiyi) in Chinese, summarizing the Gospel. Ricci aimed to proselytize the Mandarins of China. This treatise reached Korea as early as 1603 and was read, copied, and circulated among Korean scholars. The first outpouring of the Holy Spirit on the Koreans took place in 1779 during a multi-day seminar on Tianzhu Shiyi with eight participants in a Buddhist monastery. The participants were young scholars, the best known (today) being a 17-year-old young man named Yakyong Chung, who would later become a famous reformer and minister at court.

This group being unable to explain what it was that captured them, the participants decided to give their lives to the Lord Jesus. They swore to each other that they would refrain from worshiping idols and would no longer participate in the ancestral sacrifice ritual.

How Biblical this first revival was is shown by the text written by the aforementioned Yakyong Chung after receiving the Holy Spirit (this became a hymn in the "first church of Korea"):

"People and scholars of the world, do you know what is ridiculous? People come into the world, how many ghosts do they find? From morning to night they murmur their formulas, they throw all money and fortune at them to please them. Day and night they praise and worship them. All futile efforts to worship spirits only make people darker. Instead of worshiping lying spirits, let us believe in the God of Heaven; Lord in Heaven, look upon us who are like insects; You planted human lives in this infinite universe. If we destroy our own

knowledge and understand God's principle, shall we not see the light of God's grace forever? Human stupidity leads to worship of wooden idols; do you get blessings by bowing down to them? Do you become filial when you bow to the dead ancestors?"

These are lines that were until then unheard of and unthinkable in a Confucian state. Consequently, most of the eight "comrades of oath" died accused of treason. Nevertheless, the new faith quickly found many new professing adherents.

Only 15 years later, in 1794, after repeated requests from Korean Christians, the Chinese mission of the Catholic Church sent a Chinese priest named Zhou Wenmo (周文谟) who established Korea's first Catholic diocese. The Christians in Korea thus became Catholics. At that point, the community already had several thousand members and was suffering from massive persecution. The court was never able to eradicate these Christians entirely. The Korean Catholic Church produced countless martyrs in the years that followed. So the only fruit that remained of Matteo Ricci's work in the Far East were Korean Christians for the Jesuits in China were completely expelled from China in 1826 at the latest. Surprisingly, the main reason for professing Christianity for Korean Christians was that they firmly believed they had rediscovered the faith of their ancestors. Koreans were Israelites from the very beginning of their history in Asia.

Today, South Korea is a country with the largest Christian population in Asia at around 30%. 9 out of 10 largest single churches in the world are in South Korea.

2. They were scattered because they rebelled against their God: They were enslaved

11 Because they rebelled against the words of God, and contemned the counsel of the most High: 12 Therefore he brought down their heart with labour; they fell down, and there was none to help.

3. They came to China by Sea

23 They that go down to the sea in ships, that do business in great waters; 24 These see the works of the LORD, and his wonders in the deep. 25 For he commandeth, and raiseth the stormy wind, which lifteth up the waves thereof. 26 They mount up to the heaven, they go down again to the depths: their soul is melted because of trouble. 27 They reel to and fro, and stagger like a drunken man, and are at their wits' end.

The most famous founding legend of the Koreans, and historiographically the oldest, is contained in the book Hwan Dan Gogi (桓檀古), a text from the 13th century, as a clue to the arrival of the Korean Israelites by sea:

"Haung arrived at the head of an army of 3,000 men on Mount Taebaek, which is called God's Mountain. Today this place is called the Holy City, Hanung was also called the King of Heaven. He taught the art of agriculture there with the help of sages, of laws and other 360 things important to mankind, thus enlightening mankind for their blessing. At that time, there was a bear and a tiger who lived there and came to the Holy City to be allowed to live with the people. Hanung ordered that they should be taught the way. Their bodies and spirits were transformed by magic. Then their spirits were tamed, just as God originally created them. They were then given a bunch of mugwort and 20 heads of garlic, and it was explained: "If you feed on this for 100 days and avoid the sunlight, you will attain humanity.

Both the bear and the tiger complied for 37 days. The bear endured the entire phase and thus attained humanity while the tiger did not endure to the end, failing to achieve the desired goal. This was because both were of different types. The bear became a woman but she couldn't find a mate so she prayed in the forest that she might get pregnant. Hanung took the form of Han (桓) and married the bear woman who gave birth to a son. Hanung, the king of heaven, sacrificed to heaven, and the people multiplied, they were instructed in religion, and in the book of heaven, and in the doctrine of God. The people willingly obeyed. From that point on new farmland was developed, copper and iron mined to raise an army and develop the economy.

So the 9 Han (九桓) assumed the ancestors of the 3 Shin (三神, 3 gods) as common ancestors, administered the sacred places together with all other tribes, gave common laws and thus became a unit. They ordered life and wisdom, the land became perfect. From that point on, 9 Han (九桓) were led by the 3 Han (三韓) and the leader of the country, the Son of Heaven, was appointed Tan Jun Wang Jian (檀君王儉)."[1]

Particularly striking in this saga is the title of the new leader, Tan Jun Wang Jian (檀君王儉). Literally translated the title means: "Dan Prince King of modesty". "Dan" is the Hebrew word for judge (hence the name Daniel means "God my judge"). If Israeli tribes met somewhere at any time and chose a leader, wouldn't they call him a "judge" as was the case in the Old Testament in the Book of Judges? The fact that the new leader takes on the title "Dan" at least makes one take notice. Although he is at the head of the state, he is by no means a "sovereign" like the Sun King of France. He is a "humble" king.

What could the bear woman stand for? One could explain this by the fact that the royal family of the state of Chu (楚) had the surname Xiong (熊), meaning bear. The 9 Han would have been the inhabitants of the state of Chu. The State of Chu could have allied with the newcomers to gain dominance in China. Both recognized the common root as children of Jacob and thus formed a common state which, as in Canaan, was ruled by a judge (Dan).

Significantly, until early 500 BC, the capital of Chu was called Danyang (丹陽), the City of Judges, located in what is now Xichuan County, Henan Province. 9 Yi is the self-designation of the 9 Tribes of Northern Israel. For 3 Han (三韓) one could put forward the thesis that it is the self-designation of the inhabitants of Judah as "the 3 tribes of Canaan", consisting of the tribes of Judah, Benjamin and Levi. Another possibility is that 3 Han stands for kingdom of the Shem "Three" in Korean is read "Sam", from here Shem is not far.

This legend could describe the arrival of 3,000 Israelites, made up of Judah's population, from India to China, specifically in the area around Shanghai, around 500 BC. They met their fellow people from northern Israel, who called themselves 9 Yi, i.e. the 9 tribes of northern Israel.

Chinese sources show many Israelite traces of the ancient Koreans.

3.1 Levirat

The levirate, or marriage by in-law, is an ancient Israelite tradition in which the deceased's brother marries his widow. It is prescribed in the Old Testament and was also widely followed by the Israelites until the fall of both states. Levirate is first mentioned in Genesis 38:6:

"6 And Judah took a wife for Er his firstborn, whose name was Tamar. 7 And Er, Judah' firstborn, was wicked in the sight of the LORD; and the LORD slew him. 8 And Judah said unto Onan, Go in unto thy brother' wife, and marry her, and raise up seed to thy brother."

Strikingly we find references to the levirate in Chinese history books in states only which are generally considered to be ancient Korean states. Thus the levirate appears in describing the state of Fuyu (夫餘), namely in Hou Han Shu (後漢書), Book 85, Treatise on Dongyi (東夷), Fuyu (夫餘):

"Their customs are very severe and their penalties draconian and if anyone receives the death penalty all family members become slaves and if anyone steals he must pay 12 times the fine; and if someone commits adultery both the man and also the woman killed. Women who become jealous are hated; they are killed and their corpses are thrown on mountains without burial. When a man dies his brother takes his sister-in-law for his wife."[2]

A similar description of the Fuyu custom is also found in Tongdian (通典), a historical work written between 766 and 801:

"Their penalties are draconian and if someone kills they are killed and all family members are enslaved and if someone steals they have to pay 12 times the fine and if they commit adultery or if the wife gets jealous they are all killed. If a When a man dies his brother takes his sister-in-law as his wife, a custom known from the northern barbarians (北狄)."[3]

The Levirate also appears in connection with accounts of the state of Goguryeo (37 BC to 668 AD). The History of the Southern Dynasties (Nanshi, 南史, written between AD 643 and 659) states about Kaojuli (高句麗, 고구려):

"When a person dies they are buried but without a coffin, there is just an outside coffin. Funerals are celebrated on a grand scale, so much gold, silver, and jewels are used as grave goods. After the funeral service they build a burial mound out of stones and pine, and pine trees are planted. When a man dies a brother of the deceased takes the widow as his wife."[4]

In the history of the Liang (Liangshu 梁書, written around 629 AD) one finds the same text as Nanshi about Gaojuli 高句驪, in book 54, Tongyi peoples (東夷諸戎).

3.2 The Asylum Cities

The cities of asylum, or places of refuge, are called the 6 Levitical cities in the kingdom of Israel and the kingdom of Judah where persons could flee to who had accidentally killed someone. Exodus 21 describes these places of refuge as follows:

"12 He that smiteth a man, so that he die, shall be surely put to death. 13 And if a man lie not in wait, but God deliver him into his hand; then I will appoint thee a place whither he shall flee."

In the Chronicles of the Three Kingdoms (San Guo Zhi 三國志), Book Wei, Book 30, Dong Yi (東夷), book of Han (韓傳) it says:

"Because they strongly believe in spirits, they choose one man from each place to entrust him with leading the sacrifice to the sky god (天神). Each of these states also has special places called Sotu (蘇塗). There they put up a big tree, hang bells and drums on it, and serve the demons. People from all directions come here for refuge and gather here and do not return. They love to steal. The purpose of establishing the Sotu (蘇塗) is similar to that of building Buddhist monasteries so that some of the residents are good and some are rather bad."[5]

The Chronicles of the Three Kingdoms (Sanguo Zhi 三國志) was written in the late 3rd century, well after the Spring and Autumn Period. The Han (韓) mentioned here are the descendants of the 3 Han or 9 Yi of the Spring and Autumn Period. They have preserved their (Israelite) tradition of their ancestors. Apparently the tradition of the places of refuge is a tradition that is not otherwise cultivated in other places of China so that this is a feature worth reporting for the author of Sanguo Zhi. He also associates the places of refuge with religious rituals. This is not dissimilar to Jewish tradition. The rabbinic writings saw all cities of the Levites as cities of refuge where religious rituals took place.

The Later Han Book, Hou Han Shu (後漢書) is an abbreviated version of this passage.

There, Sotu is only mentioned as a place of religious ritual without mentioning the aspect of the place of refuge. This book covers a period between 25 and 220 AD but was not written until the 5th century.

"In each country they choose one man from each place to entrust him with the direction of the sacrifice to the god of heaven (天神). They call him the prince of heaven (天君) and they also set up Sotu (蘇塗). There they put up a big tree, hang bells and drums on it, and serve the demons."[6]

In the Book of Jin (Jin Shu 晉書) which refers to a later period, namely between 265 and 420 AD, one can read:

"In each country they choose a man place to entrust him with the direction of the sacrifice to the sky god (天神). This they call sky prince (天君). And they choose a special place and call it Sotu (蘇塗). They hang bells and drums on a big tree. The meaning of Sotu (蘇塗) is the same as that of the word "temple" in the West. There are good and bad people there."[7]

In these 3 texts, 3 Han (三韓) is clearly treated as an ethnic group living in many states. 3 Han is also described as part of the Dongyi (東夷) ethnic group.

3.3 Sukkot: The Feast of Tabernacles (Leviticus 23:34)

Ancient Koreans set up many asylum places in their early days where refugees found protection. These places were planted with hibiscus trees, and festivals were held there for five days, reading from the holy book, the Torah, and singing hymns. The heavenly God and the hibiscus (rose of Saron) were praised through the hymns. Such a festival couldn't be more Israelitish or biblical. The Feast of Tabernacles was probably celebrated here (Leviticus 23:34). And how they praised the Heavenly God is testified by the following text:

"Yua (於阿) Yua (於阿), Great God of our ancestors, God full of grace; All of us from the Bida Kingdom (倍達國) in the hundreds and thousands, will never forget [you].

Yua Yua, good hearts have become a great bow, evil hearts have become a target;

We, the people in the hundreds and thousands, are united and together form the bowstring of the great bow, good hearts are together and form a straight arrow.

Yua Yua, all of us in the hundreds and thousands are a great bow, aiming at many targets that are like snow clumps from evil hearts, amid boiling water from good hearts.

Yua Yua, we are all in the hundreds and thousands, an arch, have a strong heart in common and are the glory of the Bida kingdom.

Your mercy lasts for hundreds and thousands of years, O great God of our ancestors, O great God of our ancestors."[8]

Yua (於阿) could be a phonetic transcription for Jehovah (יְהוָה), Bida (倍達) could stand for Bethel (בֵּית־אֵל, House of God). The line *"Yua Yua, all of us in the hundreds and thousands are a wide arch, aiming at many targets that are like lumps of snow from evil hearts, amid boiling water from good hearts."* reminds one of Zechariah 9:13

"When I have bent Judah for me, filled the bow with Ephraim, and raised up thy sons, O Zion, against thy sons, O Greece, and made thee as the sword of a mighty man."

3.4 The name Chaoxian: Shoshan

Chaoxian, or Joseon in Korean reading, could correlate with the Hebrew word "shoshan שׁוֹשַׁן ", the flower lily, which is mentioned in Song of Song 2: 1 as a symbol of Israelites in dispersion:

"I am the hibiscus (chabatseleth חֲבַצֶּלֶת) of Sharon and the Lily (shoshan שׁוֹשַׁן) of the valleys."

Für die zerstreuten Juden war die Lilie ein identitätsstiftendes Symbol.

The Israeli shekel coin (Figure 29) has an image of a lily on the reverse. It is modeled after the first Jewish coin from Babylonia, which was minted by Jewish traders in the age of Antiochus VII (138-129 BC). The coin bears the inscription "IHD" in ancient Hebrew letters, which reflects the name of the Tribe of Judah (Yehud).

The crown of the founding king of Korean state Bohai (Korean Balhae, 699 to 719), Dae Joyeong (大祚榮), unmistakably shows the lily as the main motif (Figure 2). The portrait was painted by members of the Tae clan in South Korea, who consider themselves to be descendants of the Balhae royal family. For this portrait, they compiled all the information and materials they still had.

Figure 1 One Shekel Coin

Figure 2 Portrait of King Dae joyeong of Balhae

4. They became great for God blessed them

33 He turneth rivers into a wilderness, and the watersprings into dry ground; 34 A fruitful land into barrenness, for the wickedness of them that dwell therein. 35 He turneth the wilderness into a standing water, and dry ground into watersprings. 36 And there he maketh the hungry to dwell, that they may prepare a city for habitation; 37 And sow the fields, and plant vineyards, which may yield fruits of increase. 38 He blesseth them also, so that they are multiplied greatly; and suffereth not their cattle to decrease.

Large Israelite states emerged in China that bear the names of the 12 tribes.

In the time of Marco Polo (around 1300 AD): China consists of two large states: Kitai and Mangi, with Katai accounting for one-tenth and Mangi accounting for nine-tenths. About Mangi he writes:

„*You will be amazed at what I am going to tell you now. There are 1,200 towns throughout Mangi. In each stands an imperial garrison; you should soon find out how big such a thing is. It is guaranteed that every city is guarded by at least a thousand men; in some cities ten thousand, twenty thousand, even thirty thousand men are stationed; it is impossible to determine the total number precisely, it is far too large. Don't think that the guards are all Tartars; they are people from Catai. Not all are mounted, they are mainly foot soldiers. The garrison troops are part of the Great Khan's army. All in all it can be stated: the province of Mangi has the highest weight and mighty importance in the Tatar empire. Anyone who has never been there simply cannot imagine the wealth that lies here and the incredibly high tribute paid to the Great Khan.*"[9]

What is this supposed to mean?

Katai refers to Khitan (契丹), the people who founded the Liao (遼) Dynasty (907 – 1125). Khitan itself could stand for Gilead גִּלְעָד, the name of a grandson of Manasseh

(Numbers 26, 29). To which tribe could Mangi refer?

Manchu Yuanliu Kao (滿洲源流考) reveals that the name Manchu was not originally a territory name but a tribal name:

"Today it is written as Manchu (滿洲) in Chinese characters, but since the character Zhou (洲) denotes specific places, their territory and folk name became associated. In reality, however, it is a tribal name and it can be assumed that it is not a place name."[10]

According to Manzhou Yuanliu Kao, the Manchu people are ancient people of the Chinese continent which can be documented as early as in the times of Confucius, i.e. in the 6th century BC. These people had a variety of names throughout history.

In the beginning they lived as the Sushen tribe (肅慎氏); after that they were named in the Han period as Sanhan (三韓),
in the Wei (魏) and Jin (晉) period as Yinlou (挹婁),
in the Yuan Wei (元魏) period as Wuji (勿吉), in the Sui-Tang (隋唐) period they lived in the kingdoms of Mohei (靺鞨), Xinluo (新羅), Bohai (渤海), Baiji (百濟).

In the Jin (金) period they lived as the Wanyan tribe (完顏部)." [11]

Taking this passage into Israelitish context it reads: The Manesse tribe originally lived under the name Sushen tribe (肅慎氏, k Sukshin), the people of the Israelite flower lily (Shoshan), then in the Han period they were called as Shem Kings (Sanhan (三韓, k Samhan)), in the Wei (魏) and Jin (晉) period as Hebrew (Yinlou (挹婁, k Eubru)), in the Yuan Wei period it joined the Malchiel tribe (Wuji (勿吉, k Mugil)), in the Sui - Tang period they lived in the kingdoms of the tribes of the Malchiel (Mohei (靺鞨, k Malgal)), the Shelah (Xinluo (新羅, k Shilla), Pharez (Bohai (渤海, k Balhae)), and Becher (Baiji (百濟, k Baekjae).

Manchu, therefore, is a representative name for all the tribes of Israel, Manasseh. These people were the royal house of the last Chinese dynasty.

5. They were destroyed again and again

> 39 Again, they are diminished and brought low through oppression, affliction, and sorrow. 40 He poureth contempt upon princes and causeth them to wander in the wilderness, where there is no way.

There are large flows of refugees from China. These refugees are strong enough to found new empires again.

176 BC: Yuezhi = Yudah: migrate to Central Asia and found Sogdia in Samarkand and Kushan in northern India.

200 AD: Xiongnu = Chionite = Zionists = Huns. They founded the Hephthalite Empire in Central Asia, the White Hun Empire in Persia, reached Western Europe under the leadership of Atilla and founded many large states, such as France (Merovingians).

What does Korea stand for? It could stand for Korah from the Tribe of Levites.

Goryeo was a large empire as indicated by the worst wars they fought against Chinese empires:

Against Sui: 598 to 614: With more than 1 million Soldiers on both side.
Against Tang: 645–668, with 500,000
Against Mongols: 1231 to 1273.
Against Qing (Manchu): 1636–1637.

All these wars took place in China, not on the Korean Peninsula.

The name Karen could also derived from the word Goryeo = Kaoli in Chinese.

Today there is a huge mountainous area in western China on the border with Myanmar called Kaoli = Goryeo.

Karen and Korea are remnants of the destroyed Goryeo (Kaoli) empire. There are many common cultural heritage between Koreans and Karen.

- Naming according to the star time of the newborn baby. - Hanging peppers when a son is born.
  - Dances and Children's play games.

6. Korean and Karen history is a testimony to the faithfulness of God

42 The righteous shall see it, and rejoice: and all iniquity shall stop her mouth. 43 Whoso is wise and will observe these things, even they shall understand the lovingkindness of the LORD.

The existence of the Korean and Karen peoples is evidence that God is trustworthy.

Psalm 118, 17: I shall not die, but live, and declare the works of the LORD.

This is the credo and mission of these two peoples in our time.

Footnotes

[1]. Kim, Hoyoung (ed.), Hwan Dan Gogi (桓檀古記), Shingyochulpansa, 2013, p. 4. 4

[2] 其俗用刑严急, 被誅者皆没其家人為奴婢. 盜一責十二. 男女淫, 皆殺之, 尤治惡妒婦, 既殺, 復尸於山上. 兄死妻嫂. Hou Hanshu (後漢書), Book 85, 東夷, 夫餘.

[3] 用刑嚴急, 殺人者死, 沒其家人為奴婢. 竊盜一責十二, 男女淫, 婦人妒, 皆殺之. 兄死妻嫂, 與北狄同俗. Tongdian (通典), Book 185, Tongyi 東夷, Fuyu (夫餘).

[4] 其死葬, 有槨無棺. 好厚葬, 金銀財幣盡於送死. 積石為封, 列植松柏. 兄死妻嫂. Nanshi,

南史, Book 79, Tongyi (東夷), Gaojuli 高句麗. 6

[5] 信鬼神, 國邑各立一人主祭天神. 名之天君. 又諸國各有別邑. 名之為蘇塗 立大木,

縣鈴鼓, 事鬼神. 諸亡逃至其中, 皆不還之, 好作賊. 其立蘇塗之義, 有似浮屠,

而所行善惡有異. San Guo Zhi (三國志), Book Wei, Book 30, 東夷, 韓傳. 7

⁶ 諸國邑各以一人主祭天神, 號為"天君". 又立苏涂, 建大木以縣铃鼓, 事鬼神. Hou Han Shu, Book 85, Dong Yi 東夷, 3 Han 三韓.

⁷ 國邑各立一人主祭天神, 謂爲天君. 又置別邑, 名曰蘇塗, 立大木, 懸鈴鼓. 其蘇塗之義,

有似西域浮屠也, 而所行善惡有異. Jin Shu 晉書, Book 97, 4 Yi, 3 Han 三韓. 8

⁸ 於阿於阿我等大祖神大恩德 倍達國我等皆百百千千勿忘 於阿於阿善心大弓成惡心矢的成 我等百百千千人皆大弓絃同善心直矢一心同 於阿於阿我等百百千千人皆大弓一衆多失的貫 破沸湯同善心中一塊雪惡心 於阿於阿我等百百千千人皆大弓堅勁同心倍達國光榮 百百千千年大恩德我等大祖神我等大祖神. Lee Am (李嵒), Dangunsegi (檀君世記 단군세기), 2. Dangun, 扶婁. 9

⁹ Marco Polo, Die Wunder der Welt, p. 223 f..

¹⁰ 今漢字作滿洲 盖因洲字義近地 假借用之 遂相沿耳 實則部族而 非地名 固章章可考也.

Manzhou Yuanliu Kao, Book 1, 滿洲, p. 50. 12

¹¹ 自肅慎氏以後 在漢為 三韓 在魏晉為 挹婁 在元魏為 勿吉 在隋唐為 靺鞨

羅 渤海 百濟諸國 在金為 完顏部. Manzhou Yuanliu Kao, Book 1, Introduction, p. 37. 13

References

Hou Han Shu 後漢書, Chinese Text Project, https://ctext.org/hou-han-shu

Jin Shu 晉書, Chinese Notes, http://chinesenotes.com/jinshu.html

Kim, Hoyoung (ed.), Hwan Dan Gogi (桓檀古記), Shingyochulpansa, Seoul, 2013.

Lee Am (李嵒), Dangunsegi (檀君世記 단군세기), Übersetzung Chung, Hyuchul, Seoul, 2017.

Manzhou Yuanliu Kao (滿洲源流考), MZYLK, Chinese Text Project, https://ctext.org/wiki.pl?if=gb&res=239786. Korean Translation: Nam Chu Seong, 흠정만주원류고, Seoul, 2010

Marco Polo, Die Wunder der Welt – die Reise nach China an den Hof des Kublai Khan, 7. Aufl., Berlin, 2016.

Nanshi, 南史, Chinese Notes, http://chinesenotes.com/nanshi/nanshi079.html.

San Guo Zhi (三國志), Chinese Text Project, https://ctext.org/sanguozhi

Tongdian (通典), Wiki Source, https://zh.wikisource.org/wiki/通典.

Ethnic Mizos in Northeast India, Myanmar and Bangladesh - Recognized in Israel as 'Bnei Menashe'

by Dr PC Biaksiama

Christian Research Centre, Aizawl, Mizoram, India

Ladies and gentlemen, first of all, I want to express my deep appreciation to all the concerned scholars who devoted their time to make this symposium a reality, and I am thankful to the organizers, especially to Mrs Margot Crossings who made it possible for me to attend this meeting. I will take this opportunity to present the fact that the ethnic Mizos belong to the lost tribes of Israel and have incontrovertible evidence of affinity with the people of the book.

Let me first introduce myself as one of the foremost opponents of the claim of my ethnic Mizos as one of the descendants of the lost tribes. I once forcefully engaged with the proponents of the lost tribes in debates and I had written two books on the topic, arguing that the Mizo tribes are not from the lost tribes of Israel. But there's a sea of change now. More and more people are realizing the fact that the remote ancestors of the Mizo tribes could be traced back to Israel. More evidence is coming forth to back it up. And I am going to throw light on the history of the lost tribe and the present condition in Mizoram.

THE FIRST LIGHT OF ISRAELISM AMONG THE MIZOS

The first realization or awakening of the Mizo tribes as belonging to one of the lost tribes of Israel was initiated to the Mizo tribes almost a hundred years ago in visions and dreams. Unfortunately, before the society and the church could pay due regard to promote the evidence and fan the consequent interest, it was snatched away by a religious fringe group who marginally lived and carried on extremist views in remote villages such as Buallawn in the 1940s and early 1950s. They claimed to be the descendants of Menasseh or Manasia or Manmasi in Mizo. They made it as their newfound faith to the extreme and those who did not accept them were treated as outsiders, so, they set themselves up as a separate socio-economic and religious group away from mainstream society. In fact, their behavior and actions made them social and religious outcasts from Mizo society. They no longer worshipped in Christian churches as they separated from any Christian church, and denied Christ and Christianity. That caused great confusion to the masses of the people. They adopted Judaism as their newfound religion and they ostracized themselves from mainstream Mizo culture and set themselves as a separate group. Then they felt that they were living in a strange land and that they longed to return to their homeland, that is, Israel.

Thus, the pioneers of Israelism among the Mizos made themselves unpopular by following other religions and by making themselves strangers in a land of their own at a time when Christianity in Mizoram was in its infant state. The church leaders had no alternative but to look upon them as non-Christians (which is their true position). They no longer belonged to the Mizo church which is central to Mizo society. Separated from mainstream Mizo society by their lifestyle, the general public and educated classes looked down upon them. Unfortunately, a negative social stigma was attached to them.

This created a barrier between mainstream Mizo society and the nascent Mizo Israelism. Since Mizo Israelism unfortunately fell into the wrong hands, it turned the peoples' opinion against Mizo Israelism from the very beginning. It was a non-starter. However, a revival of interest came from another quarter.

MRS ZAITHANCHHUNGI AND 'ISRAEL MIZO IDENTITY'

The first and foremost modern researcher and writer of the history of the Mizo tribes and their connection was carried out by Mrs Zaithanchhungi (RIP), a longtime friend of Mrs Margot Crossing who lived in Mrs Zaithanchhungi's house whenever she came to Aizawl, the capital of Mizoram. Mrs. Zaii's in-depth research has resulted in the discovery of the existence of close resemblances that the Mizos had with the ancient Israelites. Her book "Israel-Mizo Identity" has produced sufficient evidence to prove that the Mizo tribes now living in northeast India and the adjoining regions of Myanmar and Bangladesh could be the descendants of the lost tribes of Israel, especially the tribes of Menasseh and Ephraim. Some of the glaring examples of the Israel Mizo identity based on her findings are given below:

1. Belief in the Almighty God. Before Christianity entered Mizoram, the ancestors of the Mizos had already believed in the only one Almighty God, Creator of

everything, whose abode is high up in heaven. This belief is similarly shared by the Israelites. This may be attributed to the reason why the Mizo people throughout the centuries could not be influenced by any other religions though they lived in the midst of Hindu majority in India, Muslim majority in Bangladesh and Buddhist majority in Myanmar.

2. Belief in Paradise or Pialral in Mizo. The Mizos believed in life after death. The soul of a man leaves his body at death for the spirit world. The spirit world is believed to have two compartments: the more luxurious compartment is called Pialral which is meant for those who had accomplishments in life whereas, the rest of the souls of the dead would go to 'Mihi Khua' (village of the dead, where life is dull and colorless. In the same manner, we see the Jews also believed in the existence of Sheol (Heb), or Hades (Gr), the shadowy existence, equivalent to Mihi Khua. In the same manner, the Jewish belief in Paradise is roughly equivalent to Mizo 'Pialral' – an existence for the privileged souls.

3. Manase/Manasia or Manmasi. One of the most outstanding examples of the Mizo community's close relationship with the Jews is the popularity of Menasseh among the Mizos since ancient times. In many of the chants used in various sacrifices, and in other sacred occasions, the name of Manasia or Manase is often used. We know Joseph had two sons, Ephraim and Menasseh. From this, it is difficult to escape the conclusion that Israel's Menasseh and Mizo Manasia or Manase are the same person. For example, when the jungles are cleared for a new settlement, the Mizo priest, before cutting the first tree would chant saying, "You are obstructing our grandfather Manasia." On other community sacrifices, the Mizo people often address themselves, "We are the children of Manasia." Naturally, the Mizos claimed to be the children of Menashe.

LOST BOOK PARCHMENT

According to the oral tradition, the Mizos claim that God gave them a written language on parchment, but they did not take care to keep it, and a dog ate it up, so they lost the book. This tradition of a lost book is common to other South Asian communities.

Though there are other examples of noteworthy similarities between the cultures of Israel and those of the primitive Mizos, let it be suffice to say. The pioneer scholar and researcher, the late Mrs Zaithanchhungi has written several books on the subject. She concluded her book as follows:

> "Similarities in laws, customs, and religious practices, some even almost identical, are so numerous that anyone who concludes they are a mere coincidence could be accused of being unable to reason. Can all these similarities be coincidence!? In fact, careful research shows that the MIZOS are the 'MENASSEH TRIBE,' one of the Lost ten Tribes of Israel." (Israel-Mizo Identity, p. 115).

On 30th March 2005, in a historic decision, the Sephardic Chief Rabbi Shlomo Amar, decided to formally recognize the Bnei Menashe of northeastern India as "descendants of Israel."

Today, over 4000 people from Mizoram and Manipur in NE India known as Bnei Menashe who claimed to be the lost tribe had migrated to Israel, and some more are sll awaing for migraon to their so-called motherland.

REASONS FOR NO GENERAL ACCEPTANCE BY MIZO PEOPLE

Due to the above stated nonstarter, there has been no general acceptance among the Mizo people that they belong to the descendants of the lost tribes of Israel because of its mishandling at the hands of the wrong people. As such, the subject had not been properly introduced in the initial stage, and the general public had not been informed from a Christian perspective, which is important in the context of the Mizos who are predominantly Christians. As such, the general public are not fully aware of the facts presented by the researchers and others, and that's the reason why, it is yet to receive wider acceptance among Christian Mizos living in Mizoram and elsewhere. Why do I state this? Let me first give my reasons:

1. Mizo are well entrenched in Christianity as the only true and righteous religion. But Mizo-Israelism has been associated with Rabbinic Judaism, and that's the reason why the issue had become unpopular among mainstream Mizo Christians.

2. Those who claimed to be the descendants of Mennaseh were taught to forgo Christianity and to adopt Judaism. This practice is anathema to the Mizos.

3. They teach among themselves that they don't belong to this land of their forefathers, Mizoram, saying that their true home-land and their final destination is Israel. It's a pity that they consider Jesus Christ as an impostor. So, they converted from being Christians to non-Christians – to Rabbinic Judaism after denying Christ and the church and the Mizo culture.

A NEW AND CHRISTIAN APPROACH TO MIZO ISRAELISM

There is an ingeniously new and encouraging approach to the Mizos as one of the lost tribes of Israel that is potentially acceptable to the Christian population of the Mizos. It comes from the well-researched manuscript on the topic written by Mrs Margot Crossing titled "The Restoraon of the Kingdom of Israel." She asked me to translate it into Mizo, and I did it without first knowing the contents of her thesis. The book surprised me and changed my mind so much that it made me a believer now. I want to explain how and why this change of mind came to be.

RESTORATION OF THE KINGDOM OF ISRAEL by MARGOT CROSSING

I am going to review this book and give my personal testimony out of it.

First and foremost, she approaches the thesis of the lost tribes of Israel from a deep Christian conviction. Her book attempts to demonstrate that one need not convert to Judaism simply because he believes that he belongs to the lost tribe. Quite the opposite is the case. Rather, the whole truth is a Christian message – an evangelical Christian message at that. Those Mizos who taught to convert to Judaism by forsaking Christianity were false teachers of the worst kind. They had done a great harm and disservice to the Mizo-Israel cause. This is certainly lamentable. Mrs Margot felt the need to tell those Mizos "NOT TO CONVERT TO JUDAISM," but to confirm the Israeliteness of their Christianity.

On the contrary, it is not only possible, but it's most desirable for a Christian to know that he belongs to the same nationality that Jesus Christ himself belonged to when He came into the world. The author, Mrs Margot, said that all over the world, wherever the Gospel of Jesus has been preached, those societies who gladly welcomed the message are always the descendants of Israel. This is exactly what happened among the Mizos. When the Gospel of Jesus Christ was introduced and preached to the Mizos in the early 20th century, they readily welcomed it and accepted it so that in record time of five decades only, the gospel spread like wildfire into the entire length and breadth of Mizoram and its neighboring states. At one point, the Mizos claimed to be 100 percent Christian before non-Christian outsiders had come in.

Mrs Margot painstakingly highlighted other communities that welcomed the Good News wherever it was introduced – in Central Asia, in China and Japan, in many parts of Myanmar such as the Karen people, the people of the Chin Hills and the different ethnic tribes in NE India, because Christianity had so many parallel traditions and cultures with the ancient Israelites.

What does Mrs Margot mean by the Restoration of the Kingdom of Israel? To discover the lost tribes and bring them into the extended communities of Israel – this will result in the joining together of the ten lost tribes of Israel's Northern Kingdom of Israel who disappeared on record in 721 BC with the southern Kingdom of Judah who also had been dispersed in different parts of the globe after the fall of Jerusalem in 70 AD. God had specific reasons for dispersing His people and sending them into all the nooks and corners of the world. According to Mrs Margot, the dispersal of His chosen nation throughout the world for two to three millenia had resulted in the co-mingling of Israelites with almost all different races of the world, so much so that by now, we can imagine that every family on the earth has some small trace of DNA from the tribes of Israel being pushed through migrations, natural growth of population and by inter-marriages with all the races.

How and why they moved from place to place were determined by local wars, famines, and migrations from place to place unto the ends of the earth. God's promise to Abraham, that is, to possess everywhere he put his feet must have some legal ramifications as his prophesied descendants – as numerous as the stars in the heavens. So, nobody including the Mizos can say with any meaningful evidence that his blood is free from the DNA of the tribes of Israel. Mrs Margot mentions the names of numerous nations who had close affinities with Israel through their cultures, and needless to say, the ethnic Mizos are one of them.

How does the author Margot Crossing try to achieve the restoration of the kingdom of Israel is most appealing to the evangelical Christian and has captivated my heart. It is to be done through Christian means, that is, by evangelizing the heathen into Christianity. Following the Great Commission of Christ, one can achieve the dual purpose of witnessing Christ on the one hand, and this very same means can serve to achieve the restoration of the Kingdom of Israel by connecting both the Northern Kingdom representing the Gentile nations with the House of Judah, the Southern Kingdom. Thus, this objecve had been perfectly accomplished among the Karen tribes in Myanmar, the Mizo tribes in NE India, the Mikir, the Khasi, and all of you who are here today, and the process is progressing well.

Now, the Mizo people have a high regard for anything Israel. After all, 80% of our Holy Bible speaks about Israel. The future of the world and especially the future destiny of our biblical faith revolves around what is happening and what will happen to Israel. Whenever there are wars in Israel with the Arabs and now, with Palestinian Hamas and Hezbollah, hundred percent of the Mizos are with Israel. We see there is a golden opportunity opening to impress upon the people about the fact that the remote ancestry of the Mizos are nobody other than God's chosen and blessed nation of Israel. The peoples' attitude could change overnight if properly presented at the appropriate me. I also personally believe the time has come for the nation of the Mizos to realize our true ancestry that will determine our future. Without a doubt, this is God's appointed time, and we are humble witness of the revealing of the divine plan of the ages. Halelluijah Amen!

Let us conclude by invoking Psalms 22:27-28 - All the ends of the earth will remember and turn to the LORD, and all the families of the nations will bow down before him, for dominion belongs to the LORD and he rules over the nations.(NIV)

A Book for All Peoples by Richard Hewitt (Risbek)
Chiang Mai, Thailand Symposium May 10th, 2024

Many years ago, I visited a high mountain village in the Tien Shan range. This village had been a winter camp for three nomadic Kyrgyz tribes before the Soviet Union's iron fist descended there. When I arrived, I asked some teenage boys if they would take me to the one elder who knew their culture better than anyone else in town. They led me to an old man who knew their history and traditions better than anyone else. I asked the old man about a Kyrgyz God-guest tradition. He confirmed what I had seen and heard: Kyrgyz believe God could be present anywhere and they anticipate His arrival. You never know which guest is the One, so Kyrgyz must constantly be ready to host God - God in human form.
I then asked the elder if I could show him this Kyrgyz tradition from Genesis 18 in the Ancient Book. He said he wouldn't touch the book for fear of offending his ancestral line and polluting his descendants.

The holy book I presented was the ancient text that intersects Kyrgyz culture with an odd familiarity. Despite this familiarity, this book is considered foreign by many Kyrgyz influencers and their foreign sponsors. This particular script has impacted the world like no other, shaping modern and traditional nations alike, outlasting empires and unending streams of enemies. The elder's animosity is common throughout the world.

Then I asked the elder if he would permit me to read their God-guest tradition from the feared, religious text. He agreed as long as he didn't have to touch the ancient book. As I read, he listened intensely about a fellow nomad named Abraham who noticed someone passing by. Abraham recognized the man as God and then welcomed God and his angelic companions to his camp. Abraham then had the fattened calf slaughtered just as Kyrgyz would. Detail after detail of this God-guest meeting mirrored Kyrgyz customs. There was one exception in the Script's version: Abraham washed God's feet. Kyrgyz wash their guests' hands. Everything else in this passage of the ancient Script precisely reflected what the old man knew about his cherished traditions.

The elder was so intrigued that he eventually grabbed the "cursed" book from me to verify that the story I was reading was actually in the book. He had heard of Abraham and knew world religions well enough, but he had never seen a holy book that captured the essence of Kyrgyz culture like this particular portion of the great Script. He begged me for the book, but I grabbed it back and read him a story from Genesis 32 paralleling Kyrgyz beliefs. Once again, he pulled the book from me to verify the text was actually there and then insisted that I give him the book. Since it was my personal copy, I respectfully took it back.

Later, I sent him a copy, and years after that, I met him again. In secret, he thanked me profusely for the book and considered it the holy book of Kyrgyz folk religion, *Tengirchilik*. We didn't share a common religion, but we had a common faith. I'll let you decide which is more important. This particular man found his own folk religion in a script that most people falsely isolate as Jewish or Christian.

High in the Tien Shan Mountains the Book fits perfectly into the ancient *Tengir* beliefs of semi-nomadic Kyrgyz. I believe this book achieves the impossible by representing the heart of every faith. It is not a human creation. It is Earth's Script. The Islamic Quran also recognizes core sections of the book as "early revelations of Allah (God)" or Allah's Early Books. The Quran commands Muslims to believe these early revelations (Surah 2:285). Additionally, in 2020, Japanese Shinto priests traveled to Israel to understand why their faith aligns with this same Script. Native Americans have customs that match the Good Book's customs perfectly, causing many European colonists and early Americans to view Native Americans as one of Israel's lost tribes. Similar stories have been repeated in China, Southeast Asia, and Africa. Ancient versions of the Script's original mid-Bronze Age alphabet have also been found in regions as far away as the Americas and East Asia. How did this book which has become the basis for modern law in many democratic nations also form the basis of so many indigenous cultures and faiths?

In the Book, it is written that:

> Your offspring will possess the nations and will resettle the desolate cities. Fear not… For your Maker is your husband - The Lord of Armies is his name - the Holy One of Israel is your redeemer. He will be called God of all the earth. "For the Lord has called you back like a wife deserted and grieved in spirit, like a wife of one's youth that is rejected," says your God. (Isaiah 54:3-6)

Humanity has strayed far from our path. Now, like an estranged wife or a runaway, we're recollecting our loving father and responding to a familiar call to return. The One known as the God of one nation, Israel, is making Himself known as the God of all nations. He is the ancient God of each ethnicity. In His own words:

> It is not enough for you to be My Servant raising up the tribes of Jacob and restoring the protected ones of Israel. I will also make you a light for the nations, to be My salvation to the ends of the earth. (Isaiah 49:6)

There is a light for all nations and a salvation to the ends of earth. The Hebrew word for that salvation is pronounced: "yeshua". If this Great Script is associated with this servant's light, then we should expect that servant to resonate with each culture. I have written that there is one man who fits this expectation. Millions consider him the Messiah of Judaism, the Mesikh of Islam, Christ of Christianity, the Kydyr or Wanderer of Central Asia's Tengir faith, Peace Child of cannibalistic Sawi, and refer to him by a whole concoction of holy names in Buddhism and Hinduism. There seems to be no end to the crosscultural, messianic roles of the first-century teacher named Yeshua.

Maybe all we need to do is translate the text into every language, change the cover for each tribe, and use local versions of the characters' names, like Ibragim instead of Abraham, for any context. Then we should leave and let the book and the Spirit do their own work, as was done with the elder in Kyrgyzstan's high mountain village.

Iconic Bible Chapters about Israel's Return by Richard Hewitt (Risbek)

This list of iconic chapters about the prophesied Israel's Return is written to help those investigating the historical, biblical, and anthropologic significance of Israel's Lost Tribes. The chapters listed here are taken from the books of the Hebrew Prophets, which are found in the Tenakh or Hebrew Bible, known to many as the Old Testament. These chapters not only foretell the return of Israel's "lost" tribes but also highlight a messianic role in the tribes' redemptive return. Jewish theology recognizes that Israel's return is woven into the foretold revealing of God's Messiah.

Large portions of prophets' writings were warnings to Israel about a coming judgment, which included exile from the homeland. The warnings weren't obeyed and the judgment fell. I didn't include those chapters, because today I am simply presenting the most iconic "Return" chapters, focused on Israel's return. I won't take time to distinguish why many don't view Israel's spectacular 1948 formation as the fulfillment of these particular prophecies.

To understand the prophets' semantics, one must understand a brief history: Israel had been a 12-tribe confederation that broke in two during the reign of King Solomon's son, Rehoboam (c. 980 BCE). Ten tribes in the north gathered around Joseph's tribes and/or the tribe of his son Ephraim. They kept the name Israel for their new ten-tribe confederation. The southern tribes were known as Judah, after their most prominent tribe. Most scholars accept that today's Jews are descendants of this southern tribe, Judah. The northern tribes, however, became "lost" sometime after Assyria deported them (c. 740 - 720 BCE).

Isaiah 11
This chapter about the return starts in Isaiah 10:20 and then detours into the destruction of Assyria who had attacked Israel. The prophecy picks up again in Isaiah 11:1 where we read that **a shoot of Jesse will come forward**, having the **Spirit of the Lord on him**. Jesse is David's father, so we can assume that this refers to a descendant of King David. There are many prophecies about the Messiah coming from David's lineage. David, Son of David, or Second David are all titles for the Messiah. Verses 4 and 5 depict the Shoot of Jesse as a **righteous judge**. Again, this imagery is

messianic. I want to highlight again that the shoot of Jesse will be characterized by the Spirit of the Lord.

Isaiah 11:6-8 portrays savage animals living as if tamed, beside what would otherwise be their prey. "**The wolf will dwell with the lamb**" is an image of peace in the messianic age within this iconic chapter about the return of Israel's Lost Tribes. That is the theme of this paper: iconic messianic imagery within the Script's most iconic chapters on Israel's return.

Isaiah 11:9 continues with the theme that **no one will hurt or destroy on God's holy mountain**. Why this extreme peace? The Script says **the earth will be filled with the knowledge of the Lord**. And so we see that "Knowing the Lord" is key to the teaching of humanity's primary candidate for the Script's Messiah (John 17:3).

Isaiah 11:10-12 needs to be read in unison. Verse 10 says the Root of Jesse will be **a banner for the peoples**. Banners represent nations and go before them. The nations had been seeded with Israelites. In verse 10 these nations rally to Jesse's Root. Isaiah 11:11 is a pivotal verse often discussed in our symposiums and roundtables. This verse says the Lord will redeem **a second time**, the remnant of His people who remain. That remnant is Israel's lost tribes. Many believe Jesus referenced this when he said he would gather another flock (John 10:16). And verse 12 revisits the theme of a banner being **lifted up for the nations**, which appear to be the dispersed of Israel. This verse, like many others, blurs the line between the nations (Gentiles) and Israelites, who will gather to this banner.

Verse 13 is a famous verse about Ephraim and Judah finally making peace. In verse 14, the two fight side by side against common enemies.

The last two verses (15, 16) mention God drying up the rivers and making **a highway so the remnant of His people may return**. That remnant is the scattered tribes of Israel who did not return with the Jews when the Jews returned from captivity to Jerusalem.

Jeremiah 31
Jeremiah 31 is within the larger return section of chapters 30-33. This is perhaps the most iconic chapter of all. Chapter 31 builds to a crescendo with a burst of messianic symbolism in verse 31-34:

> "Behold, the days are coming, declares the Lord, when I will make **a new covenant** with the **house of Israel** and the **house of Judah**, not like the covenant that I made with their fathers on the day when I took them by the hand to bring them out of the land of Egypt, my covenant that they broke, though **I was their husband**, declares the Lord. For this is the covenant that I will make with the house of Israel after those days, declares the Lord: **I will put my law within them, and I will write it on their hearts**. And I will be their God, and **they shall be my people**. And no longer shall each one teach his neighbor and each his brother, saying, 'Know the Lord,' **for they shall all know me**, from the least of them to the greatest, declares the Lord. For **I will forgive their iniquity**, and I will remember their sin no more."

The emphasis on a new covenant (v. 30) acknowledges the shortcomings of the old covenant. Jesus referenced this same new covenant when he said that his blood was the blood of a new covenant.

> For this is My blood of the new covenant, which is shed for many for the forgiveness of sins. (Matthew 26:28)

Jeremiah 31 also highlights that all will know the Lord. As stated, Jesus employs this value in his teachings. He expects his followers to know him. Those who don't know him are cast out.

> On that day many will say to me, 'Lord, Lord, did we not prophesy in your name, and cast out demons in your name, and do many mighty works in your name?' And then will I declare to them, 'I never knew you; depart from me, you workers of lawlessness. (Matthew 7:22-23)

Yeshua taught that knowing him was knowing God the father:

> If you really know me, you will know my Father as well. From now on, you do know him and have seen him. (John 14:7)

Jeremiah 31 was obviously iconic for Jesus too.

Hosea chapters 1-3

Hosea chapters 1-3 capture God's broken heart in his relationship with Israel, His bride. The whole book of Hosea is devoted to this theme and is therefore a must-read for anyone diving into the Lost Tribes topic. God famously says:

> Yet the number of the children of Israel shall be like the sand of the sea, which cannot be measured or numbered. And in the place where it was said to them, "You are not my people," it shall be said to them, "Children of the living God." And the children of Judah and the children of Israel shall be gathered together, and they shall appoint for themselves one head. (Hosea 1:10, 11a)

In Hosea, God is the groom or husband and Israel is his adulterous wife. Despite her departure, He promises to take her back, saying:

> And I will betroth you to me forever. I will betroth you to me in righteousness and in justice, in steadfast love and in mercy. I will betroth you to me in faithfulness. And you shall know the Lord. (Hosea 2:19, 20)

Jesus uses the analogy of himself as the groom. When asked why his disciples didn't fast, he answered:

> Can the wedding guests fast while the groom is with them? As long as they have the groom with them, they cannot fast. (Mark 2:19)

Yeshua (Jesus) is painting of picture of himself as the Messiah. The messiah presents a massive overlap with God himself. This blurred line between Almighty God and the Anointed Messiah is consistent with the BCE prophets' portrayal, as you may have started noticing.

Isaiah 49

Isaiah 49 has been my personal favorite. I prompted ChatGPT with the following: "What messianic imagery is in Isaiah 49? Write it as an essay." Here is the surprising response I got. I made a few personal adaptations. Notice that AI recognizes that this chapter on Israel's return has messianic imagery:

Isaiah 49 is a profound chapter about the Lost Tribes of Israel, rich with messianic imagery and considered one of the Servant Songs in Isaiah's book. Passages in this chapter describe the mission, suffering, and ultimate victory of the Lord's Servant, a figure identified as the Messiah. The chapter intricately weaves themes of preordained mission, the inclusion of Gentiles, the Servant's suffering, and the universal scope of salvation.

The chapter opens with a declaration of the Servant's calling and preparation:

"Listen to me, you islands; hear this, you distant nations: Before I was born the Lord called me; from my mother's womb he has spoken my name" (Isaiah 49:1).

This verse emphasizes the Servant's mission as predestined by God, reflecting the belief that Jesus' role as the Messiah was foretold before his birth. Furthermore,

"He made my mouth like a sharpened sword, in the shadow of his hand he hid me; he made me into a polished arrow and concealed me in his quiver" (Isaiah 49:2).

This imagery of a sharpened sword and polished arrow suggests that the Servant's words and actions will be powerful and precise, which resonates with Jesus' impactful teachings.

The Servant's mission extends beyond Israel to encompass all nations.

"And now the Lord says—he who formed me in the womb to be his servant to bring Jacob back to him and gather Israel to himself... It is too small a thing for you to be my servant to restore the tribes of Jacob... I will also make you a light for the Gentiles, that my salvation may reach to the ends of the earth" (Isaiah 49:5-6).

These verses explicitly broaden the mission to include the nations (Gentiles), aligning with Jesus' messianic message of salvation for all humanity, not just the Jewish people.

The imagery of the Servant's suffering and subsequent vindication is compelling.

"This is what the Lord says—the Redeemer and Holy One of Israel—to him who was despised and abhorred by the nation, to the servant of rulers: 'Kings will see you and stand up, princes will see and bow down, because of the Lord, who is faithful, the Holy One of Israel, who has chosen you'" (Isaiah 49:7).

The Servant's initial rejection and later exaltation parallels Jesus' rejection by his own people and his eventual recognition as Lord in every nation on earth.

"This is what the Lord says: 'In the time of my favor I will answer you, and in the day of salvation I will help you; I will keep you and will make you to be a covenant for the people, to restore the land and to reassign its desolate inheritances'" (Isaiah 49:8).

This portrayal of the Servant as a covenant for the people points to Jesus establishing a new covenant through his blood, spilled on Passover.

The universal scope of the Servant's work is evident in verses 9-12, which describe the freeing of captives, providing for the needy, and regathering God's people from all over the world.

"They will feed beside the roads and find pasture on every barren hill. They will neither hunger nor thirst nor will the desert heat or the sun beat down on them" (Isaiah 49:9-10).

This imagery highlights the inclusive and universal nature of the Messiah's mission, which many believe is fulfilled through Jesus' ministry and the global spread of his message.

The chapter further emphasizes God's unwavering compassion and assurance:

"Shout for joy, you heavens; rejoice, you earth; burst into song, you mountains! For the Lord comforts his people and will have compassion on his afflicted ones... See, I have engraved you on the palms of my hands; your walls are ever before me" (Isaiah 49:13-16).

These verses reassure that God will not forget his people, and the metaphor of engraving on the palms can be seen as a foreshadowing of the nails, where Jesus bears the marks of his love for humanity.

Finally, verses 22-26 depict a dramatic reversal where the scattered and lost children of Israel return and are cared for by foreign nations, while their oppressors face judgment. This rich tapestry of messianic imagery not only affirms the servant's central role in God's salvation history but also provides a source of hope and inspiration for believers across generations.

Wow! Even AI can see all the messianic symbolism in these iconic chapters!

Ezekiel 34

Ezekiel 34 has been another favorite of mine. It starts powerfully displaying God's love for his stubborn "Lost Sheep" and His commitment to gather them from all nations and shepherd them despite all their ailments.

> "For thus says the Lord God: Behold, I, **I myself will search for my sheep** and will seek them out. As a shepherd seeks out his flock when he is among his sheep that have been scattered, **so will I seek out my sheep, and I will rescue them from all places where they have been scattered** on a day of clouds and thick darkness. And **I will bring them out from the peoples** and gather them from the countries, and will bring them into their own land. And I will feed them on the mountains of Israel, by the ravines, and in all the inhabited places of the country. **I will feed them** with good

pasture, and on the mountain heights of Israel shall be their grazing land. There they shall lie down in good grazing land, and on rich pasture they shall feed on the mountains of Israel. **I myself will be the shepherd of my sheep**, and I myself will make them lie down, declares the Lord God. I will seek the lost, and I will bring back the strayed, and I will bind up the injured, and I will strengthen the weak, and the fat and the strong I will destroy... (Ezekiel 34:11-16)

The distinction between God, the divine shepherd, and the second David as shepherd is lost a few verses later:

"Therefore, thus says the Lord God to them: Behold, I, myself will judge between the fat sheep and the lean sheep. Because you push with side and shoulder, and thrust at all the weak with your horns, till you have scattered them abroad, I will rescue my flock; they shall no longer be a prey. And I will judge between sheep and sheep. And **I will set up over them one shepherd, my servant David, and he shall feed them: he shall feed them and be their shepherd.** And I, the Lord, will be their God, and my servant David shall be prince among them. I am the Lord; I have spoken. (Ezekiel 34:20-24)

Hundreds of years later, Jesus refers to himself as the Good Shepherd. He is obviously drawing on Ezekiel's messianic language:

I am the good shepherd. The good shepherd lays down his life for the sheep. He who is a hired hand and not a shepherd, who does not own the sheep, sees the wolf coming and leaves the sheep and flees, and the wolf snatches them and scatters them. He flees because he is a hired hand and cares nothing for the sheep. I am the good shepherd. I know my own and my own know me, just as the Father knows me and I know the Father; and I lay down my life for the sheep. And I have other sheep that are not of this fold. I must bring them also, and they will listen to my voice. So there will be one flock, one shepherd. (John 10:11-16)

Jesus knew the Prophets well. In the context of these iconic chapters, Jesus' statements are extremely bold. He also aligned his disciples with the

Ezekiel 34 prophecy when he told his friends not to go to anyone but the Lost Sheep of Israel (Matthew 10:6)

Ezekiel 36
Ezekiel Chapter 35 detours from the promising return of Israel's tribes into the judgment of Edom, but Ezekiel 36 loops back to the theme of return, promising that the Israelite cities will be rebuilt and repopulated with Israelites who had profaned God's name among the nations. God promises to cleanse them is filled with an outpouring of the Holy Spirit:

> And I will vindicate the holiness of my great name, which has been profaned among the nations, and which you have profaned among them. And the nations will know that I am the Lord, declares the Lord God, when through you I vindicate my holiness before their eyes. I will take you from the nations and gather you from all the countries and bring you into your own land. **I will sprinkle clean water on you, and you shall be clean** from all your uncleannesses, and from all your idols I will cleanse you. And **I will give you a new heart, and a new spirit I will put within you. And I will remove the heart of stone from your flesh and give you a heart of flesh. And I will put my Spirit within you, and cause you to walk in my statutes** and be careful to obey my rules. You shall dwell in the land that I gave to your fathers, and you shall be my people, and I will be your God. (Ezekiel 36:23-28)

Like so many of these iconic chapters proclaiming Israel's return, this one also has a prophecy about the messiah's work, restoring hearts of stone and giving His Spirit to his cleansed children.

Ezekiel 37
Ezekiel 37 has two important visions, both iconic in their own way. In the first vision, Ezekiel, who is called the Son of Man, sees a valley of dry bones scattered everywhere. He is told to speak life over the bones and then tells the breath (spirit) to breathe life into them. Then the bones, which are the scattered children of Israel, come together and then come back to life.

A messianic interplay can be seen in Ezekiel's title, "Son of Man" (37:9).

> Then he said to me, "Prophesy to the breath; prophesy, son of man, and say to the breath, Thus says the Lord God: Come from the four winds, O breath, and breathe on these slain, that they may live."

God gave Ezekiel the title. The prophet Daniel uses the phrase when he describes a glorious being as the Son of Man:

> "I saw in the night visions, and behold, with the clouds of heaven there came one like a son of man, and he came to the Ancient of Days and was presented before him. (Daniel 7:13)

Daniel's use of the title, "son of man", is a picture of the Messiah. Later, Jesus as Messiah, uses the title for himself, which may have been his way of saying he is the messiah who will bring life and unity back to the scattered and "dead" bones of Israel.

> "For the Son of Man came to seek and to save the lost." (Luke 19:10)

This first vision in Ezekiel 37 also states that God's Spirit will be with Israel when they return. Those of us here at this symposium, who believe we are Israelites who have returned to God, have an obligation to be filled with God's Spirit.

The second vision in Ezekiel 37 is about two sticks, one called Judah and the other Joseph. Each is named after one of the two divided nations in Israel. God will unite the two:

> say to them, Thus says the Lord God: Behold, I am about to take the stick of Joseph (that is in the hand of Ephraim) and the tribes of Israel associated with him. And I will join with it the stick of Judah, and make them one stick, that they may be one in my hand. (Ezekiel 37:19)

The Israelites will return and be united with Jews (Judah). The text also states, that David will be their unifying king and that God will make an everlasting covenant of peace with his people when he brings them back and unites them. As stated earlier, all this is messianic imagery.

Isaiah 54

The next section is from Gork, X.com's AI. The prompt was: "Write an essay on the messianic symbolism in Isaiah 54." Gorks essay didn't highlight verse 13, which says "Your sons will learn from God." That is an important verse. Additionally, I would have added verse 7, "For a brief moment I forsook you, But with great compassion, I will gather you." Verse 7 shows the turmoil of God's own broken heart. Here is Gork's response:

Title: The Messianic Imagery in Isaiah 54: A Divine Love Story

In the vast and complex narrative of the Bible, Isaiah 54 stands out as a chapter rich in messianic imagery, offering a profound glimpse into the relationship between God and His people. This chapter is a love story, a divine romance, where God is portrayed as the faithful husband and Israel as the beloved bride. The imagery used is deeply symbolic, drawing on the ancient tradition of covenantal love to illustrate the unbreakable bond between the Divine and His chosen people.

The chapter opens with a call to rejoice and sing, a call to the barren woman to enlarge her tent and prepare for a multitude of children. This imagery is reminiscent of the promise made to Abraham, that his descendants would be as numerous as the stars in the sky. It also echoes the New Testament's depiction of the Church as the bride of Christ, with the promise of a multitude of spiritual children.

The chapter then moves into a declaration of God's enduring love. The imagery shifts from a marriage to a divorce, with God as the husband who has temporarily abandoned His wife. This imagery is powerful and poignant, reflecting the historical reality of Israel's exile and God's apparent absence. Yet, the chapter ends with a promise of reconciliation and restoration. God, the husband, will return to His wife and renew His covenant of love.

This imagery of God as the faithful husband and Israel as the beloved bride is deeply messianic. It anticipates the coming of the Messiah, who will restore the relationship between God and His people. In the New Testament, this imagery is fulfilled in the

Messiah, who is described as the bridegroom and the Church (or His Community) as His bride. The love story of Isaiah 54 is a foreshadowing of the divine love story that will be fully realized in the coming of Jesus.

The chapter also contains imagery of a new creation, with the promise of a new Jerusalem and a new covenant. This new creation is also a messianic theme, anticipating the renewal and restoration that will come with the Messiah. The promise of a new Jerusalem is a promise of a new world, a world where God's love and justice will reign supreme.

In conclusion, the messianic imagery in Isaiah 54 is a powerful and poignant depiction of the relationship between God and His people. It is a love story, a story of a faithful husband and a beloved bride. It is also a story of restoration and renewal, anticipating the coming of the Messiah who will restore the relationship between God and His people and usher in a new creation. This chapter is a testament to the enduring love of God and His unwavering commitment to His people.

Not a bad summary for Artificial Intelligence.

Conclusion
Both Canonized Jewish scripture and AI engines conclude that God has prioritized the return of Israel's tribes in conjunction with the unveiling of the Script's anointed servant, the Messiah, who was chosen to bring these tribes back to God. Jesus' use of imagery from these iconic return chapters reveals that he boldly proclaims himself as that anointed Messiah.

These chapters are presented with the hope that the audience and readers will study these chapters and develop their own insights from within their own cultural context.

Did Ancient Israelites Form Eastern Religions? (Part I)
By Richard Hewitt (Risbek)

Introduction

Eastern and Western thought, often perceived as antithetical to one another, developed from a common root during the First Millennium BCE's formative years. Israelites were forcefully moved east in the 8th Century BCE. This particular diaspora became the Saka or Shaka nomads of Central and South Asia. For our purposes, they were one branch of Israel's famed "Lost Tribes," scattered among Eastern nations. A few hundred years later, the biblical stage also moved east from Israel to Babylon. Babylon was then conquered and absorbed by Persia. Eastern sages like Siddhartha and others shared the limelight with biblical prophets, characters, and events. In this expansive Persian context, seemingly incompatible faiths sprung from close proximity to one another and shared a common history.

In this essay, I suggest the founders of Eastern religions are Israelite descendants from the first Israeli diaspora that moved to and was eventually deported to the East from the 900s BCE to the 700s BCE. After this initial diaspora prepared the "soil", Eastern religions formed in conjunction with later biblical events within Babylon and then more specifically within Persia's Achaemenid Empire (559-331 BCE), including its surrounding trade partners and allies. Ironically, Siddhartha Gotama, known as Buddha, grew up within the shadow of Persia's great empire and under the influences of the same biblical prophets, texts, and events which eventually inoculated Augustine and many sculptors of Western thought. These influential prophetic texts were canonized in the West but not in the East.

The 1st Millennium BCE

The Israelites' long history as slaves in Egypt, culminated with the Exodus under Moses. They were given the Torah with its well-defined laws, stories, civil codes, and methods of governance. Their military exploits in their conquest of Caanan are still known 3500 years later. All that to say, the Israelites were highly developed before the 1st Millennium BCE began.

Israel's King David and King Solomon were at the helm of Israel's advanced civilization when the 1st Millennium BCE started. Together, in alliance with the Phoenicians (biblical Tyre and Sidon), they brought Israel to its zenith, suppressed two superpowers, Egypt and Assyria, and built Solomon's Temple, which was one of the great wonders of the ancient world.

Sadly, Solomon's later years were marked by spiritual decay and sin's divine consequences: God promised to tear ten of the twelve tribes from Solomon's dynasty. After Solomon's passing, ten northern tribes separated themselves from Judah in the south. The northern kingdom kept the name Israel and is also known by their prominent tribe Ephraim or Joseph. The South was known by its prominent tribe, Judah. According to the Script (Bible), the northern tribes (Israel) had a propensity to turn away from God to foreign gods and traditions. The Script's God called this unfaithfulness adultery, so He divorced Himself from Israel.

The Era of Prophetic Writings (900s - 400s BCE)

In the context of this divided nation, an era of biblical prophets and their sacred texts was birthed. Today, this prophetic section of the Good Book is called The Prophets. These unique Hebrew Prophets started calling the inhabitants of Judah and Israel to reform their ways, seek justice, and turn back to the God of their forefathers. If the people didn't return, the prophets said God would scatter or "sow" Israel among all nations. Similar calls to reformation and justice were central to Siddhartha's message and the teachings of Confucius and other Easterners.

The prophets' fascinating proclamations were written, transmitted, and eventually canonized in the West. Their interesting lives and eccentric actions were recorded. One eccentric prophet wasn't allowed to cry when his wife died. Another had to go naked through the city as a sign that the people would be stripped. One had to publicly lie on the ground on one side for a year as a visual lesson for the people. Their eclectic lives are still mirrored by many Eastern teachers.

Mechanism for Sowing Israelites Across the Globe

The northern kingdom of Israel didn't return to God or heed the warnings. Instead, they became corrupt and weak, so inhabitants left the kingdom. Maritime Phoenicians, who were allied with Israel, used Israelite refugees to populate Hebraic Carthage and other colonies. Phoenicia was only comprised of two city-states and didn't have a large population with which to populate their colonies. As if divinely orchestrated, the maritime Phoenicians and Carthaginians were the perfect mechanism for sowing fleeing Israelite "seeds" to distant coastal colonies around the Mediterranean and Atlantic, fulfilling the promise that they would be sown among the nations.

Other groups of Israelites fled Israel's corruption, instability, taxes, coups, and abuse by traveling overland to Semitic Urartu in modern-day Armenia. Those who wanted to keep their horses would have chosen this overland route as opposed to the Phoenicians' maritime route. The highly civilized nomadic Scythians burst into history from Urartu at this historic moment. Like Carthage, Urartu was Semitic, and like the Carthaginians, the Scythians could only have been populated primarily by Israelite migrants from Israel's shrinking population. Fast-moving, horseriding Scythians could not have been a better mechanism for sowing Eurasia with small Israelite camps that dotted the landmass. Biblical prophets had said God would sow Israel like seed among the nations, and sure enough, many city-states suddenly appeared in history as Israel's population fed into these two "seeding machines". One could say that nations, cultures, and religions germinated and sprouted around the world during this epoch.

Culturally, the Scythians could only have come from a sophisticated populace with technical skills, management, and military background. They were highly civilized even though some Westerners typify them as savages. The population probably developed their skill, technology, and finesse while building Solomon's empire and temple. Scythians were not from undeveloped Siberia as many scholars hypothesize. They quickly moved from their home in Urartu (modern-day Armenia) and skillfully planted small, civilized nomadic tribal groups from China, Siberia, and Mongolia and into Europe and the Middle East.

Assyrian Deportation (740-720 BCE)
Since David and Solomon's military power had been divided, diminished, and dispersed, Assyria slowly reclaimed dominance. From 740 BCE, the Assyrians started attacking Israel and deporting its citizens. Assyria finally conquered Israel's depopulated capital, Samaria, in 722 or 721 BCE. The Script says captives were taken to Hara, Habor, Halah, the river Gozan, and cities of the Medes on Assyria's Eastern borders.

Hara could be the Indus Valley Civilization, previously called Harappa or Harappan. Bukhara on the Silk Road also has Hara or Khara as its root. In Hebrew, the city Habor is Khyber, like Afghanistan's Khyber Pass. And by 600 BCE, the Medes occupied the birthplace of many Eastern religions - territory as far east as modern-day Afghanistan, Uzbekistan, and Pakistan, which brings us to Kashmir, Northwest India, and the Indus Valley. To this day, Kashmir, NW India, and the Indus Valley are not only known as the birthplace of many Eastern Religions but also as hotspots for the Lost Tribes of Israel and home of the former Saka people.

Birth of the Saka People (700s BCE)
History suddenly introduced the formidable Saka (Sak, Sacea, or Shaka), also known as Eastern Scythians. The Saka, like their Western Scythian counterparts from Urartu, sprung into existence quickly. They dominated their region, Central Asia at the gates of Earth's most populated areas, China and India. Steven M. Collins (1995) and George Moore (1861) are two of several scholars who brilliantly trace the emergence of the Saka from Israel's deported captives, claiming that Sak comes from Isaac. (Interestingly, my Kyrgyz name, Irisbek, also drops the initial "I" and becomes Risbek, just as Isaak became Sak.) The timing, geographic location, ethnonym, skills, culture, and habits of the Sak in Central Asia also match what scholars expect from Israel's deportation.

There is also a long list of scholars and authors who have reported on the presence of Israelites east of the well-established Saka origin or Afghanistan and Kashmir. Moving east, I've documented the Israelite roots among ethnic Kyrgyz. A slew of 19th-century missionaries have reported an Israelite presence in Asian communities as far east as China's Sichuan Province and Myanmar in Southeast Asia. Margot Crossing and Don Richardson documented several ethnic groups who have legends of a Lost Book in Southeast Asia. Crossing identifies these tribes as ancient Israelites. At our most recent symposium, Damir Eraliev presented a relational link between ethnic Kyrgyz and Southeast Asian tribes which is recorded in the Epic Manas. Professor Manasseh Pasupuleti, George Moore, Dr. Ha-Sung Chung, and others have documented Torah traditions within Eastern Religions. Arimasa Kubo and Dr. Kengo Nagami highlight an ancient Israelite presence shaping Japanese Shintoism. Dr. Ha-Sung Chung and Esther Chen trace Israelites in China. Evidence of a powerful Israelite presence in Asia is overwhelming. The Saka and Scythians seem to have been the "seeder" through which Israelites were sown into Asia.

As Assyria weakened, the Israelite-Sakas were free to move further east into the Indian subcontinent, China, and beyond to the Far East and Southeast Asia. Eastern ideologies and religions were either birthed or matured in Saka regions. Siddhartha Gotama (Gautama) Buddha was even from the Shakya clan, a name that could easily be derived from Saka/Shaka. That takes us to the primary question of this essay: were Siddhartha Gautama, Confucius, the authors of Hindu Vedas, Zoroaster, and other Eastern reformers descendants of Israel's northern tribes?

Era of Formation (1000 - 400 BCE)
All over the world, massive city-states, ethnic groups, national identities, religions, and philosophies formed from 800 BCE to 400 BCE. Were these new city-states and worldviews forming around the dispersion of Israel's tribes? One of the Script's prophets said,

> ... you will spread out to the right and the left; your descendants will dispossess nations and settle in their desolate cities. (Isaiah 54:3)

David Diringer, author of *The Alphabet, A Key to the History of Mankind* (1968), wrote:

> In the 6th century BCE, an amazing religious revolution took place in northern India. It was so powerful that it changed history. In many respects, it was a nationwide reaction to crude religious customs and blood sacrifices, which were exclusively carried out by members of the Veda priestly clan. India's two sons—Bodhidharma, the founder of Zen, and Gautama, the founder of Buddhism—were the agents of this revolution. (Volume 2, p. 260)

Indian states were falling and rising. Migrants, expanding to the left and right, were pouring onto the subcontinent from Saka regions like Bactria, Kashmir, and the Indus Valley. These migrants dispossessed Indian states and rulers and inhabited desolate cities that shaped modern India, China, Japan, Korea, Southeast Asia, Central Asia, and much more. It was nothing short of a revolution.

Babylon, Persian Achaemenids, and Jewish Captives (600s - 400s BCE)

The Scythians decimated Assyria (circa 678 BCE) in an apparent revenge attack, but Babylon dealt the final blow to Assyria's capital, Nineveh, and assumed authority over Assyria's kingdom in 612 BCE. Trade and movement between allies in the eastern border regions would have been fairly fluid, especially as the territory switched hands. Former Israelites would have been free to push east across modern-day India or northeast into China and beyond.

After Babylon took Assyria, King Nebuchadnezzar attacked the southern kingdom of Judah (597 BCE) and deported Jewish captives east. This second major diaspora did not end the era of biblical prophets. As a consequence, the Script (Bible) has pre-exilic, exilic, and post-exilic prophets. Ezekiel and Daniel are exilic prophets who continued to call God's people to return to God during Babylon and Persia's rule. Zechariah also started prophesying in Babylon/Persia, but eventually migrated back to Jerusalem and is now listed as one of the post-exilic prophets.

The prophet Jeremiah, a pre-exilic prophet, had foretold that Jews would be in Babylon for 70 years. When those 70 years were completed, Persia's Achaemenid Empire destroyed Babylon (539 BCE), allowing the Jewish return to Jerusalem. The Script follows the history of those who returned. Israelites, who were deported by Assyria over 200 years before, didn't return with the Jews. They eventually became "lost" among the nations. Post-exilic prophets prophesied in Judea during Achaemenid rule. The Achaemenids and the prophets ended after Alexander the Great annihilated Persia.

Before finishing this section, let's remember that the Persian culture, sown with Israelite seed and watered with Jewish Prophets, provided a unique context for Israelite "seeds" to germinate and sprout. Now, many centuries later, Eastern worldviews stand like giant trees with long histories. This paper revisits the origin of these massive Eastern religions.

Kings and their Decrees (600s - 400s BCE)
Babylonian and Persian kings used an additional vehicle to spread God's message in the East by making decrees that promoted Israel's God. Persia's Jewish captives had made a splash in their new home. Several Jews rose to prominence in the Babylonian and Achaemenid courts. Notable biblical figures like Daniel, Esther, Mordecai, Nehemiah, and others served influential Persian kings. Other Jews made history by taking an unpopular stance against the prevailing culture. Booklets like Daniel, Esther, Ezra, Nehemiah, and Ezekiel were written or took place within Persia. Eastern kings living with these God-followers and their prophecies often honored Israel's God enthusiastically.

The royal decrees would have been read and studied by Jewish dignitaries, Israel's long-lost tribes, Eastern nobility, Eastern reformers, and Eastern scholars like the men who taught Siddhartha. Yes, Eastern sages would have been familiar with Babylonian and Achaemenid decrees that praised the biblical God in multiple languages to countless conquered nations during their mighty eras. If the famed Eastern sages were from the first Israelite diaspora, the God mentioned in these decrees may have tugged at an ancestral memory, recalling an era when earlier prophets had warned their forefathers. The Prophet Ezekiel, speaking on God's behalf, said:

> I will scatter you among the nations and disperse you throughout the lands. I will purge your uncleanness from you. You will be defiled in the sight of the nations. Then you will know that I am the Lord. (Ezekiel 22:15,16)

If we believe the Script's God, we can assume he was fulfilling this prophecy.

Babylonian King Nebuchadnezzar (reigned from 605-562 BCE)
After a powerful showdown between Nebuchadnezzar and a few Jewish exiles who refused to bow to a new Babylonian god, Nebuchadnezzar conceded and exclaimed:

> "Blessed be the God of Shadrach, Meshach, and Abed-nego, who has sent His angel and delivered His servants who trusted in Him! They defied the king's edict and gave up their lives rather than serve or worship any god except their god. Therefore, I hereby decree that any people, nation, or language that says anything slanderous against the God of Shadrach, Meshach, and Abed-nego will be torn limb from limb and their house made a pile of rubble, because there is no other god who can deliver in this way." Then the king promoted Shadrach, Meshach, and Abed-nego in the province of Babylon.

King Nebuchadnezzar: To all peoples, nations, and languages who dwell in all the earth: May your peace abound! It seemed good to me to declare the signs and wonders that God Most High has done for me. How great are His signs, and how mighty are His wonders! His kingdom is an everlasting kingdom, his dominion from generation to generation. (Daniel 3)

Can you imagine Siddhartha reading that decree?

Persia's king followed suit (c. 500 BCE):
Later, King Darius wrote to all the nations and peoples of every language on all the earth:

> May you prosper greatly! I issue a decree that in every part of my kingdom, people must fear and revere the God of Daniel.
> For he is the living God, and he endures forever; his kingdom will not be destroyed, and his dominion will never end. He rescues and he saves; he performs signs and wonders in the heavens and on earth. He delivered Daniel from the power of the lions."
> So Daniel prospered during the reign of Darius and the reign of Cyrus the Persian (Daniel 6).

That is written in the Good Book… to all nations.

Artaxerxes (reigned 465–424 BCE)
The following section is cut & pasted from the Script:

> This is a copy of the letter King Artaxerxes had given to Ezra the priest, a teacher of the law, a man learned in matters concerning the commands and decrees of the Lord for Israel:
> Artaxerxes, king of kings,
> To Ezra, the priest and teacher of the Law of the God of Heaven: Greetings.
> Now I decree that any of the Israelites in my kingdom, including priests and Levites, who volunteer to go to Jerusalem with you, may go. You are sent by the king and his seven advisers to inquire about Judah and Jerusalem concerning the Law of your God, which is in your hand. Moreover, you are to take with you

the silver and gold that the king and his advisers have freely given to the God of Israel, whose dwelling is in Jerusalem, together with all the silver and gold you may obtain from the province of Babylon, as well as the freewill offerings of the people and priests for the temple of their God in Jerusalem. With this money, be sure to buy bulls, rams, and male lambs, together with their grain offerings and drink offerings, and sacrifice them on the altar of the temple of your God in Jerusalem.

You and your fellow Israelites may then do whatever seems best with the rest of the silver and gold, per the will of your God. Deliver to the God of Jerusalem all the articles entrusted to you for worship in the temple of your God. And anything else needed for the temple of your God that you are responsible to supply, you may provide from the royal treasury.

Now I, King Artaxerxes, decree that all the treasurers of Trans-Euphrates are to provide with diligence whatever Ezra the priest, the teacher of the Law of the God of Heaven, may ask of you—up to a hundred talents of silver, a hundred cors of wheat, a hundred baths of wine, a hundred baths of olive oil, and salt without limit. Whatever the God of heaven has prescribed, let it be done with diligence for the temple of the God of heaven. Why should his wrath fall on the realm of the king and his sons? You are also to know that you have no authority to impose taxes, tribute, or duty on any of the priests, Levites, musicians, gatekeepers, temple servants, or other workers at this house of God.

And you, Ezra, by the wisdom of your God, which you possess, appoint magistrates and judges to administer justice to all the people of Trans-Euphrates—all who know the laws of your God. And you are to teach any who do not know them. Whoever does not obey the law of your God and the law of the king must surely be punished by death, banishment, confiscation of property, or imprisonment.

Jews in the Achaemenid Courts

From the cut-and-paste section above, we can see that Eastern kings developed a reverence for God. Jews like Daniel, revered for his prophetic visions and wisdom, navigated the corridors of power in the courts of Achaemenid rulers, offering counsel and interpreting divine messages. Mordecai the Jew was the second-most powerful person in the Achaemenid Empire during his life.

> "For Mordecai, the Jew was second only to King Ahasuerus, preeminent among the Jews, and held in high esteem by the multitude of his people." (Esther 10).

Esther was King Ahasuerus' Jewish Queen, chosen from the prettiest girls throughout the province. She boldly addressed the king and flipped the outcome of a decree throughout Persia's many provinces. Cyrus' initial decree to rebuild God's temple shaped Persia's political climate for generations. Nehemiah was also in the courts of King Artaxerxes, inspiring the king to sponsor the rebuilding of Jerusalem with supplies, edicts, and a guard. We just read about Ezra, who played a pivotal role in the revitalization of Jewish religious practices in *Yehud Medinata*, the Achaemenidian Province of Judah. The teachings, writings, and experiences of biblical characters not only shaped the destiny of their people but also resonated throughout Persia's vast multiethnic empire and beyond. This all took place as many national identities, cultures, and faiths were solidifying.

Israelites and the Birth of Eastern Religions

With the establishment of the Achaemenid Empire over multiple cultures and trade routes, some 8th-century BCE Israelite deportees found themselves within the Achaemenid Empire together with more recent 6th-century BCE Jewish prophets and their sacred texts. They all watched empire-wide events that honored their ancient God. But did the former Israelites recognize the prophets or the God who was proclaimed? Two centuries after leaving Israel, who had the Israelites become? How would they have responded to the voices of Jewish prophets and priests? Would they have recognized the "voice" of their ancient God?

These events sparked a spiritual revival all over Asia. Remarkably, the Bhagavad Gita, the sacred Hindu Vedas, the Dhammapada and the Sutta Pitaka of Buddhism, the Avesta of Zoroastrianism, the Analects of Confucius, and the Tao Te Ching of Taoism were all written in this powerfully biblical era. The sages (many of whom were nobility) had access to the kings' decrees and the prophets' writings.

Korean scholar Ha-Sung Chung writes that a tablet was found in the Keifang Synagogue, suggesting Confucius had access to the Script/Bible (2023, p. 8). If these Eastern scholars were descended from the advanced, twelve-tribe confederation under David and Solomon's rule, they could easily incorporate spiritual concepts from the powerful God who had earned the attention of kings. Many Easterners would have been reawakened by what they were hearing.

Additionally, Margot Crossing (2019) arguing on behalf of peoples of the Lost Book claims they are scattered from Central Asia to Southeast Asia. She analyzes several cases and defends why the lost book must be the Torah or Hebrew Bible (Tenakh). She believes the nations of the East centered their beliefs and practices on the Script until the Chinese emperor Shih Huang Ti burned all books except agricultural and medical books in 213 BCE. Interestingly, this happened as Jews were canonizing their holy books in Jerusalem. Those canonized texts quote God saying,

> "This is the one to whom I will look: he who is humble and contrite in spirit and trembles at My word." (Isaiah 66:2)

When the Script was canonized, those canonized writings became foundational for Westerners.

A Few Eastern Religions from the Achaemenid Era

The following is a list of Eastern religions and a shallow snippet of their overlap with biblical values:

Zoroastrianism (628 BCE–551 BCE, Pahlavi sources)
Zarathustra's era is debated, but Zoroastrianism, one of the world's oldest monotheistic religions, was born in the 6th century BCE, during the Achaemenid period. The religion's central tenets, such as the belief in a single God, heaven, hell, and a day of judgment, parallel the Script's teachings.

Hinduism (c. 1000–500 BCE)
Hinduism, an ancient religion, coalesced during the later Vedic period (c. 1000–500 BCE). The possibility of Israelite migrations to the Indian subcontinent presents intriguing parallels with certain elements of Hinduism. For instance, the monotheism in the Vedas is no different from what the Lost Tribes would have known. Both Hinduism and ancient Israelites mixed polytheism with their monotheistic foundation.

Buddhism (500s BCE)
Siddhartha Gautama Buddha was born in 563 BCE, at the midpoint of the Jewish captivity in Babylon. The religion he started was not what it is today. Like some of his cohorts, the biblical prophets, Siddhartha Gautama was a wandering religious teacher who lived in northern India or Nepal during the 6th or 5th century BCE. Siddhartha didn't want to be worshiped. He wanted people to reform their ways and taught the Four Noble Truths and the Noble Eightfold Path.

1. The Four Noble Truths:
   - Life is characterized by suffering, pain, and dissatisfaction.
   - The cause of suffering is craving or attachment to desires.
   - It is possible to end suffering by ceasing attachment to desires.
   - The Noble Eightfold Path is the way to achieve liberation from suffering.
2. The Noble Eightfold Path:
- Understanding the Four Noble Truths and seeing things as they are.
- Developing thoughts free from attachment, ill will, and harm.
- Abstaining from lying, divisive speech, harsh speech, and idle chatter.
- Acting in ways that are not harmful to oneself or others, such as refraining from killing, stealing, and sexual misconduct.
- Earning a living in a way that does not harm others or oneself.
- Cultivating positive states of mind and preventing negative states from arising.

- Being fully aware of one's thoughts, feelings, and actions in the present moment.
- Developing deep concentration and mental stability through meditation.

Those familiar with Yeshua's teachings about God's love, denying self, forgiving others, blessing one's enemies, seeking truth, etc. will notice the overlap with Buddha's values. Jay G. Williams (2004) even suggests that Yeshua is Buddhism's "Way" to ultimate enlightenment.

Dr. Ha-Sung Chung (2021) argues that Buddhism spread quickly through the lost Israelite communities. Israelite groups may have changed their ethnic names for a variety of reasons, including fear of anti-Semitism. The Script reminds us that many Jews from the southern kingdom of Judah hid their identity when they lived in exile (Esther 2:10). Israel's diaspora likely did the same. They may have disguised their biblical faith in Buddhism.

The Tibetan Buddhist Encyclopedia[45] has an article titled "Siddhartha Gautama Buddha Prophecies Jesus" (March 2022) with fascinating references to Gautama's predictions of the "Lord of Mercies" coming with pierced side, hands, and feet. Such prophecies in Eastern religions are controversial but make sense because Zechariah and Ezekiel disseminated similar prophecies about the coming king. Zechariah, like Siddhartha, also prophesied that the coming king would be pierced. Hinduism's Vedas also contain verses about Isha Masiha (Yeshua Messiah) and the white-robed "Lord of Nations," most likely written at the same time as Zechariah.[46]

One sore verse written in the Great Script over a hundred years before Siddhartha's birth seems to shed an odd light on Buddhism. Isaiah says:

> "Those who consecrate and purify themselves to go into the grove, following one who is among those who eat the flesh of

---

[45] TibetanBuddhistEncyclopedia.com

[46] http://tibetanbuddhistencyclopedia.com/en/index.php/Siddhartha_Gautama_Buddha_prophecies_Jesus

pigs, rats, and other unclean things—they will meet their end together with the one they follow," declares the Lord."

Oddly, legend tells us that Siddhartha met his end after eating swine in a grove. I can't judge, but I also can't ignore the odd parallel of this obscure verse and Siddhartha's enigmatic death. Since Siddhartha Gautama didn't want to be worshipped, I imagine this verse is for those who disrespect him by following him as if he were God. A true Buddhist reformation would follow Buddhism to its prophetic roots and refresh the doctrines in light of a Buddhist interpretation of the writings that initially inspired Buddha.

Jainism (c. 700 BCE):
The twenty-fourth *tirthankara* Mahavira (c. 600 BCE), a noble by birth, like Siddhartha, formalized the religion's central tenets, such as nonviolence, karma, and the concept of liberation - all tenants with strong biblical ties.

Confucius (c. 551 – 479 BCE)
Confucius emerged as a preeminent philosopher whose teachings emphasized ethical conduct, piety, social harmony, and humane governance. The Analects, a compilation of Confucius's sayings and teachings, have obvious parallels to the Script.

Taoism (400s BCE)
The core of Taoist thought crystallized during the 5th century BCE around the *Tao Te Ching* and the *Zhuangzi* Texts written in that era.

Each of these major Eastern faiths developed while Israelites were being propelled across the globe and while the Achaemenids' famous kings reiterated the biblical events they witnessed. And while Jewish prophets spread their message to Jewish communities across the Achaemenid Empire and its trade routes.

> Mordecai recorded these events, and he sent letters to all the Jews throughout the provinces of King Ahasuerus, both near and far. (Esther 9:20)

All sorts of religious writings were being penned, translated, and distributed according to the practices of the Achaemenid era. Each text appears to overlap with the next. Of course, later religions, like Bahai, Sikhs, Christianity, and Islam, developed well after the First-Mellenium BCE. These younger faiths all branch off of the earlier faiths.

Conclusion

The historic, geographic, cultural, and religious context suggests that Siddhartha Gautama and other Eastern reformers were ancient Israelites from the famed Lost Tribes of Israel deported east from Israel in the 8th Century BCE. Two centuries later those Eastern tribes were inspired by a new wave of exiled Jews in Babylon and Persia. Royal decrees in multiple languages sent by messengers to over 100 conquered nations within Babylonia and Persia. The nations heard multiple royal decrees from powerful messengers honoring the biblical God for several generations. Eastern religions such as Buddhism and Hinduism formed in this context.

Part II will dive deeper into the personalities, specifics, and Eastern teachings of the biblical prophets and the messianic culmination of their foretellings. We'll examine the Magi's interpretation of the prophets, legends of Yeshua in the East, and Yeshua's dictate to his disciples to go to "the lost sheep of Israel".

Bibliography

Chen, Ester. (2012). *The Hidden Qiang, "Sons of Sheep"* (Electronic Version, Sichuan, Chengdu, China)

Chung, Ha-Sung; (2021, December 27) *How Did Buddhism Spread So Easily in the Far East? On the Relationship Between Buddhism and Israelitism.* Academia.comhttps://www.academia.edu/66108657/How_did_Buddhism_Spread_so_easily_in_the_Far_East_On_the_relationship_between_Buddhism_and_Israelitism_Discussion_paper

Chung, Ha-Sung, Dr.; Dispersion of the Israelites in the Eurasian Continent: How GOD has fulfilled His Promise: History of Eurasia from Biblical Perspective (Independently published, 2023)

Collins, Steven M. (1995). The Ten Lost Tribes of Israel… Found! CPA Books

Crossing, Margot; Lost Book Peoples; Connecting Northeast India to Central Asia through Oral Tradition, (World Epic Festival, Scientific Symposium, Bishkek, 2019)

Diringer, David. (3rd edition, 1968). *The Alphabet, A Key to the History of Mankind.* (Hutchinson of London)

Eidelberg, Joseph. (2005). *Biblical Hebrew Origin of the Japanese People* (Gefen Publishing House, Jerusalem, Israel)

Gade, Anne Katrine. (1988). Who Were the Cimmerians and Where Did They Come From? (*The Royal Danish Academy of Sciences and Letters*)

Gertoux, Gérard. (2015). *Dating the reigns of Xerxes and Artaxerxes* (researchgate.net) https://www.researchgate.net/publication/312069819_Dating_the_reigns_of_Xerxes_and_Artaxerxes (May 5, 2024)

Girard, René. (1987). *Things Hidden Since the Foundation of the World* (Stanford University Press)

Grant, Asahel; (1841) The Nestorians, Or, The Lost Tribes (Harper and Brothers)

Halkin, Hillel (2002). *Across the Sabbath River in Search of the Lost Tribes of Israel* (Boston, Houghton Mufflin Company)

Hanh, Thich Nhat; 1995) *Living Buddha, Living Christ - 20th Anniversary Edition* (Richmond Books, New York)

Hewitt, Richard (Risbek). (2006). *A Comparative Analysis of Kyrgyz Jakyb and Jacob the Prophet* (First International Festival of Epics, Bishkek, Kyrgyzstan)

Jacobovici, Simcha (Director). (2006). *Quest for the Lost Tribes of Israel* [Film, DVD release] A&E

Khalidi, Tarif; (2001). *The Muslim Jesus: Saying and Stories in Islamic Literature.* Harvard University Press.

Khuplam, Milui Lenthang. (2013). *The Wonderful Genealogical Tales of Manmasi (Kuki-Chin-Mizo).* Maxford Books.

Kubo, Arimasa (2022, July 25) "Israelites Came to Ancient Japan" https://remnant-p.com/isracame.htm

Lhungdim, David. (2021). Menashe - Manmasi the Lost Tribe of Israel (Shivtei Menashe Publications)

Mangalwadi, Vishnu. (2011). *The Book That Made Your World: How the Bible Created the Soul of Western Civilization* (Thomas Nelson)

Moore, George MD. (1861). *The Lost Tribes and the Saxons of the East and the West, with New Views of Buddhisms, and Translations of the Rocks-Records in India* (London, Longman and Brothers)

Nagami, Kengo Dr.; Author of "Japanese and Jews"; Personal communication throughout 2023

Orozbakov, Sagymbai: Manas Translated by Walter May (Bishkek, Rarity Press, 2004)

Parrinder, Geoffrey. (1995). *Jesus in the Qur'an* (Oneworld Publications, Oxford,)

Richardson, Don. (1984). *Eternity in Their Hearts* (Regal Books, Ventura, CA)

Riegert, Ray; Moore Thomas; (2003). *The Lost Sutras of Jesus* (Ulysses Press, Canada)

Schmidt, Wilhelm, (reprinted 1983) *The Origin of the Idea of God*. (University Press of America)

Shachan, Avigdor (2007) *In the Footsteps of the Lost Ten Tribes*; (Devora Publishing Company)

Torrance, Thomas; (2nd edition, 1988). *China's First Missionaries; Ancient Israelites*. (Daniel Show Publisher)

Williams, Jay G.; (1978). *Yeshua Buddha*; (The Theosophical Publishing House, Wheaton, Ill)

Zephyr, Alexander; (2013). *Rabbi Akiva, Bar Kokhba Revolt, and the Ten Tribes of Israel* (San Bernardino, iUniverse)

Zhang, et al, (2022, July 25). *A Late Pleistocene human genome from Southwest China,* Current Biology, https://www.cell.com/current-biology/fulltext/S0960-9822(22)00928-9?_returnURL

Zaithanchhungi. (2008). Israel-Mizo Identity (L.N.Thuanga "Hope Lodge")

Zi, Lao; The Analects Attributed to Confucius [Kongfuzi], 551-479 BCE; Translated by James Legge (1815-1897); (Published December 13, 1901) https://china.usc.edu/confucius-analects-12

Schedule: Thailand Chiang Mai Symposium - Bones Come Together

May 9th, 2024
10:00 a.m.
Intro Richard Hewitt

10:10 a.m.
Read Ezekiel 37:1-14 (Have local read) What scriptural imagery comes to mind as you read?

10:30 a.m.
Damir Eraliev video with Q&A
Some tribes of Manase spread from Kyrgyzstan

10:45 a.m.
Margot Crossing With Q&A
Concept of the Restoration of All Things

11:10 a.m.
Dr. Kengo Nagami with Q&A
Jesus followers moved from Central Asia to Korea and Japan
Who were the Hata? What were they doing?

11:35 a.m.
Dr. Howard Chung with Q&A
Part 1 - Israelite Migrations across Asia (Korea and Southeast Asia)

12:00 p.m Noon - Lunch

1:00 pm
 Read - John 20:19-23 (Look for connections with Ezekiel 37)

1:15 pm
Rabbi Joseph Shulam
Joseph, Don't convert to Judaism

1:35 pm
Arimasa Kubo
Even Earth's most exotic nation has Israeli roots

2:00
Margot Crossing
The Karen People & the Peoples of the Lost Book

2:30
Discussion

3:00 p.m. Finish

May 10th, 2024

10:00 a.m.
Margot Crossing
Introducing the Lost Tribes Institute

10:10 a.m. Reading Isaiah 11 Is there a messianic hint? Are there any links between this BCE passage and the CE or New Testament?

10:30 a.m.
Margot Crossing - Part 2 Restoration - Holy Spirit

11:00 a.m.
Richard Hewitt
Iconic Lost Tribe chapters in scripture with messianic & Holy Spirit references

11:45 a.m.
PS Haokip
Vision

12:00 p.m.
Lunch

1:00 p.m.
Dr. P.C. Biaksiama
Heart to Heart - Brother to Brother

1:30 p.m.
Richard Hewitt
A Book for All People

1:50 p.m.
Rededication to the Lord

2:00 p.m.
Praying for One Another

2:40
Q&A

3:00 p.m.
Finished

www.ingramcontent.com/pod-product-compliance
Lightning Source LLC
Chambersburg PA
CBHW081459040426

42446CB00016B/3311